PRIMARY SOURCES IN POLITICAL THOUGHT

T0158674

THOEMMES

LIBERALISM, DEMOCRACY, AND THE STATE IN BRITAIN: FIVE ESSAYS, 1862–1891

Edited by
Julia Stapleton

UNIVERSITY OF DURHAM THOEMMES PRESS

Published by Thoemmes Press, 1997

Thoemmes Press
11 Great George Street
Bristol BS1 5RR, England

US office: Distribution and Marketing
22883 Quicksilver Drive
Dulles, Virginia 20166, USA

Hardback : ISBN 1 85506 534 7
Paperback : ISBN 1 85506 535 5

Printed in England by Antony Rowe Ltd, Chippenham

CONTENTS

Preface   6

Introduction
   Radical Liberalism in Mid Nineteenth-Century Britain   7
   James Fitzjames Stephen and Liberal Patriotism   10
   Lord Acton: Liberalism and Nationalism   14
   A. V. Dicey: Individualism and Political Conservatism   19
   T. H. Green: Liberalism and Social Reform   24
   Herbert Spencer and the Bureaucratic State   29
   Conclusion   35

Bibliography   41

'Liberalism'
The Cornhill Magazine, V (1862), pp. 70–84
James Fitzjames Stephen   46

'Nationality'
Home and Foreign Review, I (1862), pp. 2–25
J. E. E. Dalberg-Acton, First Baron Acton   66

'The Balance of Classes'
Essays on Reform (London: Macmillan, 1867), pp. 67–84
A. V. Dicey   97

Liberal Legislation and Freedom of Contract
(London: Slatter & Rose, 1881), pp. 5–22
T. H. Green   111

'From Freedom to Bondage'
in T. Mackay (ed.), *A Plea for Liberty: An Argument*
Against Socialism and Socialistic Legislation
(London: John Murray, 1891), pp. 1–26
Herbert Spencer   135

Index   158

PREFACE

The five pieces reprinted here belong to the polemical literature of liberalism in the last four decades of the nineteenth century. They illustrate a creed whose adherents were acutely aware of its recent achievements and further potential in shaping British society and politics. The dynamic, highly reflective nature of British liberalism in this period is evident in major texts such as J. S. Mill's *The Subjection of Women* (1869), James Fitzjames Stephen's *Liberty, Equality, Fraternity* (1873), and Herbert Spencer's *The Man versus the State* (1884). However, many free-standing essays were also important in defining the contours of liberal thought when the political fortunes of liberalism were at their height. This volume represents a sample of such writing. The contributions by Acton and Green are more well known to students of nineteenth-century political thought than those by Stephen, Dicey, and Spencer. However, all the selections merit reproduction on account of their quality and significance, as well as the range of liberal ideas which together they encompass.

I am most grateful to Dr Stefan Collini for his helpful comments on an earlier draft of the Introduction, and to Mrs Janet Starkey for invaluable editorial assistance.

> N.B. (1) The page numbers in the text of the Introduction refer to the essay being discussed as reprinted in this volume.
>
> (2) Some footnotes are cumulative, giving the source of several preceding quotations where they are from the same work.

INTRODUCTION

Radical Liberalism in Mid Nineteenth-Century Britain

The dominant tone of liberal politics in the middle decades of the nineteenth century in England was set by the radicalism of Richard Cobden and John Bright. Cobden was instrumental in the repeal of the Corn Laws in 1846; under Bright's leadership, parliamentary reform took a decisive step forward in 1867 – albeit as the triumph of Disraeli's Conservative government. Both were the icons of middle-class Dissent, their political force lying in denunciation of the stranglehold of an hereditary aristocracy over Church and State to the detriment of that sense of personal worth which they insisted belonged to all members of society. Their chief hope lay in the extension of the franchise, although education and, of course, the reduction of government expenditure also loomed large in the outlook of 'Manchesterism' – as Cobden's liberalism was dubbed by Disraeli in 1848.[1] It is true that Bright feared the uncertain effects of full universal suffrage and distanced himself from the cause of democracy.[2] He confined his support for further enfranchisement after 1832 to the inclusion of 'another million or two of our people within the pale of the constitution'. Nevertheless, he combined moderation in respect of the suffrage with an optimistic belief in the imminent possibility of England's liberation from 'the prejudices and darkness of the past'. Bright succeeded in forging a united front between the middle and working classes alike – the long-suffering victims of the 'class' government of England's traditional élite. Much of the programme of Dissenting liberalism was implemented during Gladstone's first ministry of 1868–74. Then church rates and the purchase of army commissions were abolished, the Irish Church disestablished, the entry of

---

[1] On Cobden's political ideas, see W. H. Greenleaf, *The British Political Tradition, The Ideological Heritage* (London: Routledge, 1983), pp. 32–48.

[2] H. Tulloch, *James Bryce's 'American Commonwealth': the Anglo-American background* (Woodbridge: The Boydell Press, 1988), p. 26.

7

Dissenters into universities secured, and the groundwork of a national system of education laid.[3]

Beyond electoral politics, the spirit of this liberal crusade against the shackles of tradition in English society was well-captured in John Stuart Mill's essay *On Liberty* (1859). However, a notable departure from Dissenting liberalism in this work was an emphasis upon the responsibility of the lower classes themselves for the strength of custom, convention, and tradition in English society (as well as an attack upon Calvinism for suppressing the individual will that, for Mill, was so essential to personal liberty). In this, admittedly, they were merely legatees of an undistinguished aristocratic inheritance: Mill had emphasised in one of a series of early articles entitled 'The Spirit of the Age' that, since their new-found security following the Glorious Revolution, the English monarchy and aristocracy had declined markedly in terms of 'mental energy and ability'.[4] In order to attain the greatness promised by the institutions of pre-Revolutionary England, liberalism was charged with the task of loosening the hold of orthodoxy which the new holders of power had imposed on the educated free spirits in whom, in Mill's view, all hope for the future lay. This would provide the basis of the healthy alliance between the forces of liberalism and democracy which he outlined in his essay, *Considerations on Representative Government*, published in 1861. If electoral scope were given to minorities in a democratic system of government, then an élite corps of 'instructed minds' would raise the tone of political conflict between the two principal classes of employers and employees in modern society. Democracy should not be conceived on the simple majoritarian lines of Bright and his followers, with the franchise as an individual right; rather, political power was a trust to be exercised in the interests of the people as a whole.[5]

---

[3]   J. H. Grainger, *Character and Style in English Politics* (Cambridge University Press, 1969), pp. 88–94.

[4]   J. S. Mill, 'The Spirit of the Age, 3' [Part 2], *The Examiner*, 13 March 1831, in *Collected Works of John Stuart Mill* 22 (University of Toronto, 1986), pp. 278–82.

[5]   The 'medieval' nature of Mill's conception of popular sovereignty here has been stressed by M. Francis & J. Morrow, *A History of English Political*

No sooner, however, had liberalism became associated with the abolition of established institutions, conventions, and beliefs in the cause of an intellectually vigorous democracy, than argument developed anew concerning this identity. It was especially questioned whether respect for tradition was indeed incompatible with the realization of a liberal society, and whether democracy was the natural handmaiden of the latter. The belief that liberalism and tradition were inextricably linked revived, in new forms, the Whiggism of the early decades of the nineteenth century associated, for example, with Sir James Mackintosh and T. B. Macaulay. This rival to utilitarianism had stressed the nature of liberty as a secure, continuous and unique English inheritance rather than a by-product of *a priori* reasoning about human nature.[6] From the 1860s, and away from the metropolitan and provincial centres of agitation for the extension of the franchise, liberal thinkers more widely evinced a greater receptivity towards the past and assessed the merits of democracy and the nature of the state accordingly. Mill himself had made such a concession in 1859, reflecting a long-standing view of his that the best chance for Radicalism in a political sense lay with Conservatism, and vice-versa.[7] In a review article Mill agreed on one point with his erstwhile ally John Austin, whose opposition to all further parliamentary reform late in life he otherwise rejected. This was 'the importance of adapting our improvements, whenever it is possible, to the framework of the existing Consitution'. He continued, '[u]ntil mankind are much more improved than there is any present hope of, even good political institutions cannot dispense with the support afforded by traditional sentiment'.[8]

The radical liberalism of early to mid-Victorian England was not uniformly rejected by the next generation of liberals; rather,

Thought in the Nineteenth Century (New York: St Martin's Press, 1994), p. 240.

6   See S. Collini, D. Winch & J. Burrow, *That Noble Science of Politics: a study in nineteenth-century intellectual history* (Cambridge University Press, 1983), chap. 3.

7   J. H. Burns, 'J. S. Mill and Democracy, 1829–1861', in J. B. Schneewind (ed.), *Mill: a collection of critical essays* (London: Macmillan, 1968), p. 325.

8   J. S. Mill, 'Recent Writers on Reform', *Fraser's Magazine* (April 1859), in *Dissertations and Discussions: political, philosophical, and historical* 3, 2nd ed. (London: Longmans, 1875), p. 64.

it was more often modified and adapted to changing social and political conditions. In this regard, a wide diversity of aims and ideals emerged in English liberal thought in the last four decades of the nineteenth century. What is interesting, however, is the role which positive and unitary conceptions of English society and character played in shaping the various liberal responses to the more sectarian radical heritage of the first half of the nineteenth century. In turn, after 1885, when the Liberal Party's fortunes began to wane, liberalism became a defining feature of Englishness.[9] This shift can be discerned to different extents in the writings of the authors whose essays are reprinted here.

James Fitzjames Stephen and Liberal Patriotism

The piece entitled 'Liberalism' by James Fitzjames Stephen (1829–94), a stern judge and prolific contributor to leading nineteenth-century journals, represents an acerbic challenge to the radical liberalism of the Dissenting classes and their sympathizers, even during that creed's most successful decade. Written in 1862, the article presaged Stephen's stinging indictment of John Stuart Mill's liberalism, in his book entitled *Liberty, Equality, and Fraternity* (1873). That work was written following Stephen's three-year service as the Legal Member of the Viceroy's Council in India. The son of an influential colonial administrator – the Right Honourable James Stephen – J. F. Stephen constantly hailed the British empire as an outstanding moral and political feat which had made a profound impact upon English national life. In this he anticipated the ripening of Britain's imperial consciousness in the last quarter of the nineteenth century.[10] It is hardly surprising that with all the lawyer's pessimism of human nature, compounded by his sense of the need for decisive government to bring peace and security to vast and unruly

[9]   D. Smith, 'Englishness and the Liberal Inheritance after 1886', in R. Colls & P. Dodd (eds.), *Englishness: politics and culture 1880–1920* (Beckenham: Croom Helm, 1986), p. 255.

[10] J. H. Grainger, *Patriotisms: Britain 1900–1939* (London: Routledge and Kegan Paul, 1986), p. 125.

populations like those of India, Stephen scoffed at Mill's 'abstract' prescriptions for a liberal society. For Stephen, it was inconceivable that liberty could be achieved without the discipline of established rules, beliefs, and restraints, the absence of which spelt sheer 'lassitude'. Originality and creativity, that is to say, were only stimulated within a strong moral and intellectual framework in which the individual was not abandoned entirely to his own meagre resources.[11] In general, Stephen considered Mill's liberalism as soft and effeminate, oblivious to the force of coercion at the heart of all societies.

Stephen did not differ from Mill on the importance of the liberal ideals which the latter was seeking to uphold; his criticism related more to the kind of society in which they were likely to flourish, and which was, in turn, rooted in a very different assessment of human nature. As a biographer of Stephen has remarked, for all Mill's concern about the present, abject state of mankind, he was hopeful of 'the general educability and changeability of the common man'. By contrast, while Stephen saw 'great virtue in strenuous independence', he viewed 'the mass of humanity as largely open only to the effects of restraints'.[12]

Furthermore, Stephen disagreed with Mill's 'melancholy' view of English society in the 1860s, as inhibiting rather than enhancing individuality, a point which he made in his review of *On Liberty* for *The Saturday Review*.[13] Herein lies the essence of Stephen's charge against what he termed 'Manchester Liberalism' – its detestable want of patriotism, a failing it shared with Mill. That particular liberal current, together with the 'sentimental' novels of Dickens, Disraeli, Mrs Gaskell, and Charles Kingsley, which idolized the working classes and greatly exaggerated their misfortunes, raised Stephen's ire to the full. Both tendencies, according to Stephen's brother Leslie,

---

[11] James Fitzjames Stephen, *Liberty, Equality, Fraternity: and three brief essays* (University of Chicago Press, 1991), p. 87.

[12] K. J. M. Smith, *James Fitzjames Stephen: portrait of a Victorian rationalist* (Cambridge University Press, 1988), pp. 210–11.

[13] 'Mr. Mill on Political Liberty (Second Notice)', *The Saturday Review* (19 February 1859), reprinted in A. Pyle (ed.), *Liberty: contemporary responses to John Stuart Mill* (Bristol: Thoemmes Press, 1994), pp. 15–24.

'appeared as different manifestations of a paltry and narrow indifference to all the great historic aims of [English] national life',[14] they threatened to increase what Stephen depicted in his article on 'Liberalism' as the 'quiet ignoble littleness of character and spirit' then abroad, a phenomenon which, nevertheless, Stephen was satisfied had not yet become fatal (61). But to prevent any further development along these lines, he insisted that Liberalism must be concerned with the affirmation rather than the denial of national greatness – it must assume a positive direction, in place of the purely negative one it had taken recently. The true liberal politician, Stephen maintained, with classic Burkean veneration, would

> look upon himself as a man charged to introduce to his estate an heir who had attained his majority; he would teach those whom he addressed to see in the institutions of their native land neither a prison to escape from nor a fortress to storm, but a stately and venerable mansion which for eight centuries had been the home of their ancestors, and in which they were now to take their place and play their part. (54)

In accordance with this conception of liberalism, the most that could and should be expected of the 'great mass of mankind' was that of 'recognising the moral and intellectual superiority of the few who...ought to be regarded as their natural leaders, and of following their guidance, not slavishly but willingly, and with an intelligent co-operation' (60). Bestowing sovereign power on the people was likely to end all prospects of further political reform, springing as they did from conflict between the different elements in society. The process of change would terminate, just as streams in all their various manifestations disappear when they unite 'to form a calm, lowland river' (51).

Stephen's conception of liberalism was one in which both radicalism and a flaccid, morally neutral individualism had been jettisoned. Instead, the ideal of liberty was linked to the achievement of personal excellence on the part of the few for whom this was possible. Moreover, liberty entailed attainment

[14] Leslie Stephen, *The Life of Sir James Fitzjames Stephen* (London: Smith, Elder & Co., 1895), pp. 160–61.

which flowed with, rather than against, the grain of national life, ennobling the latter as a result. For all the qualms which Stephen shared with Mill about the 'tyranny of the majority' and the 'stationariness' to which it would lead, he regarded Mill's declaration of the individual's independence from society as completely misguided. In characteristically vivid language, he maintained that such a step would

> give us all the air of dwarfs, living each in a separate corner of the house which our fathers built, and congratulating ourselves on the fact that we no longer find it necessary to quarrel as to who is to give orders, or how the rooms are to be arranged. (62)

In levelling this criticism against Mill, Stephen echoed a similar view to that of R. H. Hutton (1826–97), editor of the Unitarian journals the *National Review* and the *Prospective Review*. This view was that Mill's liberalism concentrated solely upon individual liberty at the expense of social or national liberty. Mill had mistaken the homogeneity of public opinion in England for the silencing of all dissent. In reality, however, this consensus represented a 'genuine assimilation of opposite schools of thought',[15] with the decline of local and moral groups and 'class types' in religion and politics, a process that had been gathering pace during the previous century. The tolerance of all shades of opinion would merely breed indifference, and Hutton echoed Stephen's concern about the 'liberty to be a nation' to which Mill seemed impervious. Hutton criticized Stephen for belittling the value of individual liberty; for example, in the moral sphere, the ultimate goal of liberals should be 'the largest possible amount of free co-operation with the moral law', rather than the compulsory system of morality over a wide area which Stephen was effectively proposing. Human beings, Hutton argued, should not be 'driven about by hopes and fears of which [they are] the shuttlecock'; their acts must be restrained, but only when there exists a 'real moral conviction' – as opposed to conventional

---

[15]   R. H. Hutton, 'Mill on Liberty', *The National Review* (1859), reprinted in A. Pyle (ed.), *Liberty*, p. 85.

belief – that a form of behaviour is wrong.[16] Yet in the absence of what Hutton termed 'the free play of *social* opinion,...a fit instrument for the timely assertion of England's antipathies and sympathies, hopes and will', the liberty which Mill claimed for the individual would be 'a poor sort of thing'.[17]

Lord Acton: Liberalism and Nationalism

Mill also found a critic in the Liberal Catholic historian and politician Lord Acton (1834–1902). This is most famously expressed in the latter's essay on 'Nationality' which is reprinted here. However, on a different front, while suspicious of Mill's secular form of liberalism as devoid of any absolute moral ideals,[18] nevertheless Acton endorsed Mill's condemnation of coercion in matters of religious and all other varieties of belief. Reviewing *On Liberty* in 1859 in the Catholic journal *The Rambler*, of which he was the editor, Acton asserted that liberty meant 'absence of accountability to any *temporal* authority'.[19] But he further maintained that the exercise of *spiritual* authority within the Church was not subject to the same constraints. As Herbert Paul emphasized in his memoir of Acton, the latter was a position from which Acton retreated subsequently. As a prominent critic of ultramontanism *within* the Catholic Church from the late 1860s, Acton argued that an excess of spiritual authority was as equally incompatible with liberty as that of temporal authority.[20] The consequences of this shift for Acton's political thought will be discussed presently.

Throughout his life Acton's commitment to Catholicism was the determining feature of his political thought, as is evident in

---

[16] R. H. Hutton, 'Mr. Stephen on Liberty, Equality, Fraternity' (1873), reprinted in *Criticisms on Contemporary Thought and Thinkers: selected from The Spectator*, (London: Macmillan, 1894), pp. 134–9.

[17] R. H. Hutton, 'Mill on Liberty', pp. 97–8 (ed. emphasis).

[18] G. Himmelfarb, *Victorian Minds* (London: Weidenfeld & Nicolson, 1968), pp. 185–6.

[19] J. S. Mill, 'On Liberty' 1, *The Rambler* (Nov 1859), p. 68.

[20] H. Paul (ed.), *Letters of Lord Acton to Mary, daughter of the Right. Hon. W. E. Gladstone* (London: George Allen, 1904), p. xxviii.

his essay on 'Nationality'. This was a masterly analysis of the contradictory causes which that principle had served since its inception, including the ultimate end of civil freedom it was likely to promote, in spite of itself. The essay, which was published in the successor to *The Rambler, The Home and Foreign Review*, argued strongly in favour of the multinational rather than the national state as integral to liberty and civilization, as well as Catholicism. This was a direct challenge to the position which Mill had stated in his essay on *Considerations on Representative Government* and which had also been voiced by the Italian idealist, Giuseppe Mazzini – that separate nation-states were a necessary condition of free institutions.[21] Acton's response consisted of the federalist solution he applied to a range of political problems in the next few decades, notably Home Rule in Ireland and the crisis within the Catholic Church wrought by the declaration of Papal Infallibility in 1870. A plurality of nations within the state was the only safeguard against absolutism, having the same effect in this regard as the separation of Church and State. As Acton was to write in 1882, 'Liberty depends on the division of power. Democracy tends to unity of power'.[22]

In his essay of 1862, he emphasized how democracy had fanned the flames of nationalism, founded as it was upon the 'perpetual supremacy of the collective will, of which the unity of the nation is the necessary condition...' (85). This was certainly true of democracy as it had arisen in France. Nationalism, in this exclusive form, was culpable on two accounts. First, it militated against the 'ordered liberty' which had been warmly praised in Burke's political thought and which Acton enthusiastically endorsed.[23] This is clear when he wrote against nationalism that:

---

[21] J. S. Mill, *Considerations on Representative Government* (London: Longmans, 1861), chap. 16; Joseph Mazzini, *The Duties of Man* (1860; London: J. M. Dent, 1907). For an interpretation of Mazzini's nationalism which is less inconsistent with the political values of Acton, see M. Viroli, *For Love of Country: an essay on patriotism and nationalism* (Oxford: Clarendon Press, 1995), pp. 144–56.

[22] H. Paul, *op. cit.*, p. 124.

[23] D. Mathew, *Acton: the formative years* (London: Eyre & Spottiswode, 1946), p. 5

> In supporting the claims of national unity, governments
> must be subverted in whose title there is no flaw, and
> whose policy is beneficent and equitable... (86)

Equally, however, nationalism stood condemned in Acton's
eyes as the enemy of civilization, the ideal of which constituted
a keynote of nineteenth-century liberalism. He asserted that:

> Inferior races are raised by living in political union with
> races intellectually superior. Exhausted and decaying
> nations are revived by the contact of a younger vitality.
> (87)

For Acton, the result of nations forming their own states would
be that stagnation and societal reverse into barbarism which had
haunted Mill, and before him, T. B. Macaulay.

> It is in the cauldron of the state that the fusion takes place
> by which the vigour, the knowledge, and the capacity of
> one portion of mankind may be communicated to another.
> Where political and national boundaries coincide, society
> ceases to advance, and nations relapse into a condition
> corresponding to that of men who renounce intercourse
> with their fellow-men. (87)

Acton added that stronger nations must not oppress the weaker
nations in a political union; there must be a recognition of
national differences and a willingness to do justice to them. The
(Catholic) Church, he maintained, had always defended
'national liberty against uniformity and centralisation', if only
because national liberty and religious liberty were inextricably
tied. Indeed, the impetus towards multinationalism was
provided in good part by Catholicism which had discouraged
'wherever [it] could the isolation of nations'; it had
emancipated mankind from the physical and material bonds of
kin and region by promoting the concept of the nation as a
moral and political relationship with rights and duties towards
other nations. While Acton praised the Austro-Hungarian
empire for pursuing the ideal of the multinational state, he
acknowledged its failings in the sphere of religion: instead of
strengthening the independence of the Church, it had attempted
to 'bribe' the latter, as well as destroying the diversity and
autonomy of the provinces (89).

By contrast, the British State (and Empire) constituted a model of the multinational state. In this regard, Acton extolled the virtue of tradition over the state of nature, actual nations over 'abstract nationality'. The French conception of nationalism, which had issued from the revolutionary idea of the 'sovereignty of the people' was intentionally 'independent of history. It sprang from the rejection of the two authorities – of the State and of the past' (74). England, for Acton, represented an opposite stream of both liberal and national political development stemming from the settlement of 1688. In this light, he maintained that 'the nationality formed by the state...is the only one to which we owe political duties, and it is therefore the only one which has political rights' (91).

Like Stephen's attempt to unite the concept of liberty with that of rules, Acton's trenchant criticism of the doctrine of nationalism illustrates the much closer connection between liberalism and tradition in Britain after 1860 than in the radical liberalism of preceding decades. It is true, as Hugh Tulloch has argued, in his recent study of Acton, that the latter lost much of the political moderation and balance which had characterized essays like 'Nationality', after he chose to be silenced by the Catholic hierarchy rather than risk excommunication by further attacks upon the declaration of Papal Infallibility. For example, he adopted a view of history which stressed discontinuities rather than continuities, in contrast to contemporary English historians such as Maine, Freeman, Stubbs and Bryce. This is evident in his critical review of James Bryce's *American Commonwealth* of 1888,[24] which viewed the American Revolution as a simple extension of Magna Carta and the Bill of Rights, thereby denying the radical spirit of Natural Law in which the Americans had declared their independence. But according to Tulloch, Acton's dissent, in this regard was in an important sense an exercise in personal vindication, as well as a consequence of his recognition that nothing short of a revolutionary act was needed to enforce Irish Home Rule after Gladstone's proposals were rejected in 1886 and 1893:

[24]   James Bryce, *The American Commonwealth*, (London: Macmillan, 1888).

> He believed that a true liberal could entertain no reverence
> for the past, but should rather destroy great men and
> established reputations from a position of resolute
> independence, should be forever on his guard against
> every tradition and every authority...following his own
> conscience into isolation.[25]

The truth seems to be that Acton, in his later years, was torn
between two rival conceptions of liberalism and the state: one
which stressed the need for revolution as a cleansing act against
political tyranny and injustice, and had as its concomitant a
yearning for political and moral absolutes; and one which
stayed close to the ideas of Edmund Burke – despite the
contempt which Acton sometimes expressed for the latter in
later years, particularly in private correspondence.[26] This
second facet of Acton's thought continued to emphasize the
importance of political tradition and historical continuity, the
detachment of representatives from the opinions of their
constituents, and the need for multiple centres of power. The
distance which this Burkean side of Acton represented from
mid-Victorian liberalism – and, indeed, his own propensity at
this time to see history as something from which mankind
required emancipation – can be seen in his keen defence of the
House of Lords in 1881. In a letter to Mary Gladstone, he
conceded the case for 'a modification' only. The proposal

> To "sweep away" the House of Lords would be a terrible
> revolution. The more truly the House of Commons comes
> to represent the real nation, the more it must fall under the
> influence of opinion out of doors.... Now the opinion of a
> whole nation differs from that of any limited or united or
> homogenous class by its inconstancy.... Therefore, the
> more perfect the representative system, the more
> necessary is some other aid to stability... [The House of
> Lord's] note is Constancy – the wish to carry into the
> future the things of the past, the capacity to keep aloof
> from the strife and aims of the passing hour...[27]

---

[25] H. Tulloch, *Acton* (London: Weidenfeld & Nicolson, 1988), p. 81.

[26] On Acton's turning against Burke – and Whiggism – after 1870, see
Himmelfarb, *op. cit.*, pp. 187–89.

[27] H. Paul (ed.), *op. cit.*, pp. 101–102.

A. V. Dicey: Individualism and Political Conservatism

A. V. Dicey (1835–1922) was far more receptive to Mill's individualist form of liberalism than James Fitzjames Stephen, his cousin. This was despite the fact that in the 1860s, when Dicey was a barrister in London, he shared none of Mill's anxiety about the dreary and insidious uniformity of outlook that had apparently engulfed English society. It was because of his liberal individualist principles, and his belief that they were deeply ingrained within English life, that he welcomed the extension of the franchise in 1867 – support which he expressed in the piece reprinted here. This deep strain of patriotism above all distinguished Dicey from other liberal radicals in the 1860s. However, by the turn of the century he had become greatly unnerved by democracy, particularly in the light of its association with collectivism, which Dicey despised as a byword for socialism.

We can best understand Dicey's commitment to both Mill's liberalism – shorn of its pessimistic view of English society – and his democratic sympathies in the 1860s, with reference to the tremendous admiration for the English Common Law which he developed in the 1880s. *His Introduction to the Study of the Law of the Constitution* of 1885 was essentially a pæan to the common law – and the rule of law in English polity to which it had given rise.[28] This work emanated from lectures he delivered at Oxford as the Vinerian Professor of Law, a position he secured in 1882. Both the form and content of Common Law, as David Sugarman has pointed out, is permeated with the values of individualistic liberalism; the actors which that law recognizes are individuals only, hence discouraging collective interests.[29]

---

[28] On the national pride which informed Dicey's *Law of the Constitution*, see S. Collini, *Public Moralists: political thought and intellectual life in Britain, 1850–1930* (Oxford: Clarendon Press, 1991) (henceforth cited as *Public Moralists*), pp. 289–301. On Dicey's legacy in this respect, see J. Stapleton, 'Dicey and his Legacy', *History of Political Thought* 16, 2 (1995), pp. 234–56.

[29] D. Sugarman, 'The Legal Boundaries of Liberty: Dicey, Liberalism and Legal Science', *The Modern Law Review* 46 (1983), p. 108.

Dicey's perspective of English Common Law is readily apparent in his contribution to the debate about parliamentary reform, his essay entitled, 'The Balance of Classes'. It was included in a volume which expressed similar, largely enthusiastic, views by a number of prominent young liberal scholars over the issue of extending the suffrage.[30] As Hugh Tulloch has emphasized, the influence on the essayists of American solutions to the problem of parliamentary representation is striking, indicating the absence of the qualms about mass politics which troubled older liberals like Mill.[31] The question which Dicey took up in promoting the case for reform was whether political representation should be accorded to classes or individuals. He was much concerned to attack the view of Conservatives like Sir Hugh Cairns, that only classes should be represented, giving due weight to each, thus obviating the preponderance of the most numerous class – the working class. The erroneous assumption which Dicey found beneath this reasoning was that class identity defines the most essential interests of the individual. His rejection of this premise turned upon an empirical-cum-normative analysis of English society in the 1860s, that its class divisions were fluid rather than rigid; each class, moreover, being heterogenous rather than homogenous. Enfranchising orders rather than individuals would merely serve to intensify loose and ill-defined class loyalties, turning representatives into tribunes rather than members of parliament. If a class were treated thus, it would surely act as such. By contrast, he confidently proclaimed,

> [a] free extension of the franchise in 1867 will, in thirty years, make the artisans as little distinguishable from the rest of the nation as are the men whose fathers in 1832 almost overthrew the Constitution from which they were excluded. (109)

[30] *Essays on Reform* (London: Macmillan, 1867). A companion volume was issued shortly after entitled *Questions for a Reformed Parliament* (London: Macmillan, 1867).

[31] H. Tulloch, *James Bryce's 'American Commonwealth'*, p. 27. On the backdrop to *Essays on Reform*, see C. Harvie, *The Lights of Liberalism: university Liberals and the challenge of Democracy* (London: Allen Lane, 1976).

Thus, Dicey voiced a typical liberal disdain for corporate groups in society, insisting that 'there is nothing specially to be reverenced in orders or interests' (108). It was a claim which he repeated after 1875, as trade unions appeared to receive more favourable treatment under the Conspiracy and Protection of Property Act than under all previous relevant Acts. He praised the conservative interpretation put upon the Act by the courts, and deplored subsequent legislation which gave the unions what he regarded as an unwarranted position of privilege in society. The courts' view that unions could still be liable for civil action, even if they were not indictable for conspiracy seemed to Dicey commendable to all who held that 'personal liberty is the basis of national welfare'. At the heart of his disquiet with organized interests like orders and unions lay a deeply felt sense that

> *Esprit de corps* is a real and powerful sentiment; it drives men to act either above or, still more often, below the ordinary moral standard of their conduct as individuals... [The power of a body created by combination] is created by the surrender of individual liberty on the part of each of its associates, and a society may from this surrender acquire far greater strength than could be exercised by the whole of its members acting separately.[32]

This stance was wholly in keeping with Dicey's defence of the protagonists of 'so-called unphilosophic and vulgar Radicalism' – a reference to Bright – in his essay of 1867. Their cause was a worthy one, insisting, as it did, that 'each man is the best manager of his own affairs', and second, that individuals were to be regarded primarily as persons, only secondarily as members of classes (109). But for all Dicey's common sympathy with the radical liberal camp in the 1860s, he was to depart from it in two crucial respects during the next two decades, as his thought became increasingly conservative.

First, Dicey had none of Bright's animus against landed wealth. He voiced caustic remarks about the lack of testamentary freedom in France, whereby all land was to be

---

[32]   A. V. Dicey, 'The Combination Laws as Illustrating the Relation between Law and Opinion in England during the Nineteenth Century', *Harvard Law Review* 17 (1904), pp. 531, 513.

divided equally among the family of the deceased. In addition, he staunchly defended the House of Lords – with its basis in the landed aristocracy – in the wake of the Parliament Act of 1911. These responses indicate a clear respect for the existence of 'ranks' in society, albeit fluid and unorganized.[33]

Second, in keeping with his admiration for the Common Law mentioned earlier, Dicey believed that the legal profession was the ultimate guardian of English liberty, with the implication that all was not rotten in the old order. While explicitly distancing himself from antiquarianism, Dicey nevertheless saw great merit in the legacy bequethed by seventeenth-century lawyers such as Coke and Hale, in the constitutional struggles of the time.[34] This heritage was part and parcel of the Common Law defence of personal liberty which was zealously guarded by the courts. Bright had identified the state with parliament, and sought the general good of society there, once that institution was reformed. Dicey, by contrast, was apt to see the judiciary, rather than the government, as representing 'the august dignity of the state'.[35] There was no clash of liberal perspective here so long as Dicey could assume a basic conformity of individualist outlook between parliament and the courts. Once, however, later in the nineteenth century, parliament became caught in the grip of collectivist fervour, it was necessary to reiterate the primacy of the Common Law tradition in the maintenance of liberty, and to instil radical, individualist liberalism with patriotism on that basis. In his *Law of the Constitution*, Dicey had constantly alluded to the rule of law in such terms as 'that rule of law equal and settled law which is the true basis of English civilisation'.[36] In his *Lectures on the Relation between Law and Public Opinion in England*

---

[33]   A. V. Dicey, *Lectures on the Relation between Law and Public Opinion in England during the Nineteenth Century* (1905; London: Macmillan, 1940) (henceforth cited as *Law and Opinion*), p. 59. See his bitter reaction to the Parliament Act in his essay 'The Parliament Act, 1911, and the Destruction of all Constitutional Safeguards', in Sir William Anson *et al*, *Rights of Citizenship: a survey of safeguards for the people* (London: Frederick Warne, 1912).

[34]   A. V. Dicey, *Introduction to the Study of the Law of the Constitution* (1885; London: Macmillan, 1962) (hereafter *Law of the Constitution*), p. 18.

[35]   Quoted in S. Collini, *Public Moralists*, p. 296.

[36]   A. V. Dicey, *Law of the Constitution*, p. 18.

during the Nineteenth Century (1905), he rang warning bells against the creeping collectivist mentality which threatened to undermine the individualism in the English psyche and from which the rule of law had derived much of its strength in England. It was not so much democracy which he blamed for the increasing hold of socialism upon English political life. Democracy, by itself, was a benign influence which set great store by the independence of the people; by contrast, collectivism substituted for the popular will that of experts and officials who presumed to know what was best for society. Rather, the fault lay in a shift of opinion away from legislative conservatism which had been the norm in England, a shift caused by a strong but misplaced wave of sentimentalism among the middle classes and from which even members of his own profession had not been immune. In his introduction to the second edition of *Law and Public Opinion* published in 1914, Dicey wrote:

> The desire to ease the sufferings, to increase the pleasures, and to satisfy the best aspirations of the mass of wage-earners has become a marked characteristic of the wealthy classes of Englishmen. This sentiment of active goodwill, stimulated no doubt by ministers of religion, has spread far and wide among laymen, e.g. lawyers, merchants, and others not specially connected with any one religious, theological, or political party.[37]

With typical bravado, Dicey attempted to make light of this philanthropic impulse, anticipating that it would merely lead to a modification and reform of the country's institutions. He placed great faith in the deep hold that attitudes of *laissez-faire* still exerted among working and middle classes alike, an outlook which 'has kept alive emphatically the [individualist] virtues of the English people'.[38] Nevertheless, Dicey testified to the undermining of the 'manly, muscular' type of liberalism that had shaped James Fitzjames Stephen's response to radicalism in the 1860s and 1870s, ironically by the educated classes in whom Stephen and like-minded contemporaries had

---

[37] A. V. Dicey, *Law and Opinion*, p. lxiii.
[38] *Ibid.*, p. lxxi.

placed so much faith.[39] Beneath his surface confidence lay serious reservations about the direction of social and political change with the advent of democracy, the debacles of successive Irish Home Rule Bills and the Parliament Act of 1911 setting the seal upon his disillusion. He was by no means alone in considering democracy and liberalism incompatible at the end of the nineteenth century, as we shall see when we consider Herbert Spencer's ideas. Yet Dicey's individualist form of liberalism had moved substantially out of favour among intellectual liberals in the 1880s, although here – just as in Dicey's own case – the heritage of radicalism was reworked rather than cast aside.

T. H. Green: Liberalism and Social Reform

T. H. Green (1836–82) was closely in sympathy with the philanthropic strain of opinion in British politics during the last quarter of the nineteenth century which Dicey regarded as so out of keeping with the Common Law virtues embodied in traditional liberalism. Like Dicey, Green held a Chair at Oxford – the Whyte Professorship of Moral Philosophy – from 1878 until his early death four years later. Earlier, as undergraduates in the 1850s, they had been friends and associates in the Old Mortality Society. This circle formed a refuge for students with philosophical, radical, and even republican inclinations at a time when the clientele of Oxford was largely aristocratic and politically conservative. Dicey held great respect for Green and was initially sympathetic to his concern for the harsh conditions of working class life. But they went on to develop markedly divergent views of the task of liberalism in the late nineteenth century.[40]

Most of Green's philosophy, principally in the form of lectures, was published posthumously. This included his *Prolegomena to Ethics* (1883) and his *Lectures on the*

---

[39] Stefan Collini has explored this current of liberalism in relation to Henry Fawcett. See his *Public Moralists*, chap. 5.

[40] M. Richter, *The Politics of Conscience: T. H. Green and his age* (London: Weidenfeld & Nicolson, 1964), pp. 80–81.

Principles of Political Obligation (1895). The *Prolegomena* provided the moral and metaphysical framework for his political thought, including an account of the common good as the animating ideal in society and its progress from the Greek and Christian to the modern world. This, in turn, was based upon a conception of God's immanence rather than transcendence, his revelation to mankind through history and human institutions, and above all, through the modern ideal of citizenship. Green's moral theory stimulated the revival of Idealism in English political philosophy and was a conscious attack upon the hedonist and individualist principles of Utilitarianism, as well as an attempt to rescue Christianity from the seeds of doubt sown by recent biblical scholarship.[41] His writings elevated the state to a position which it had rarely enjoyed in English thought during the past century, except in the work of Edmund Burke, S. T. Coleridge and Matthew Arnold.[42] The state, for Green, was not an obstacle to, but the *sine qua non*, of personal freedom and social cohesion; it was more than the mere instrument for securing rights which it had traditionally constituted in liberal thought, being rather the highest expression of mankind's will to achieve the common good and harmony with others. Yet, as several commentators have pointed out, for all Green's positive emphasis upon the state as the focus of a moral ideal of citizenship, he made few departures from the programme of mid-Victorian liberalism. John Bright ranked high in his political esteem, as he had in Dicey's, and he would travel miles to attend radical meetings.[43] What Green did was to detach the ideal of liberty from the individualist assumptions and arguments upon which it had rested hitherto. Moreover, he attempted to do so in such a way as to justify a limited but nonetheless definite extension of the

---

[41] On the moral and religious dimension of English Idealism, see A. Vincent and R. Plant, Philosophy, *Politics, and Citizenship: the life and thought of the British idealists* (Oxford: Blackwell, 1984), chaps. 1–2.

[42] On the centrality which the state came to assume in political discourse during the last two decades of the nineteenth century, particularly in the work of liberal thinkers, see J. Meadowcroft, *Conceptualizing the State: innovation and dispute in British political thought 1880–1914* (Oxford: Clarendon Press, 1995), pp. 58–59.

[43] M. Richter, *op. cit.*, p. 82.

range of state action, sufficient to satisfy some of the more pressing reformist impulses of the day but without undermining individual motivation and responsibility.

The lecture reprinted here – 'Liberal Legislation and Freedom of Contract' – was delivered at Leicester in the summer of 1880 under the auspices of the Liberal Association. It was intended to provide a philosophical defence of recent extensions of the state by Liberal administrations, together with laws which were currently being proposed by the Gladstone government of which Bright was a minister.[44] Among the pieces of legislation whose liberal credentials had been called into question were the Ground Game Act (which denied landlords the power to claim exclusive right to game on their lands), and the Employers Liability Act, which made employers liable to pay compensation to workmen injured at work. Green noted that these and other departures from traditional liberal practice had gathered pace after the 1867 Reform Act. He welcomed this move towards democracy as evidence of further expansion of the boundaries of the common good, a process which had been under way since antiquity. At the same time, Green defended the new face of liberalism as perfectly consistent with 'the same old cause of social good against class interests, for which, under altered names, Liberals are fighting now as they were fifty years ago' (113). Nevertheless the conception of freedom which Green maintained underlay recent interventionist acts and which justified further measures too, was substantially different from that which liberals had traditionally held, that is, that freedom consists in the absence of restraint.

For Green, freedom was not to be understood as the mere doing of what one likes, nor was it a state which an isolated and independent person could realize, however elevated the objective pursued. Neither, moreover, was freedom attainable at the expense of the well-being of others. As Green argued,

> When we speak of freedom as something to be so highly prized, we mean a positive power or capacity of doing or enjoying something worth doing or enjoying, and that,

44   *Ibid.*, p. 269.

too, something that we do or enjoy in common with
others. (117)

Other contemporary liberal thinkers – like Matthew Arnold –
had similarly attacked the sense of freedom in radical,
Dissenting liberalism as doing as one likes. In his *Culture and
Anarchy* (1867–9), Arnold had maintained that freedom means
the attainment of balance and perfection through the cultivation
of the highest human faculties – in short, through the sweetness
and light of 'culture'.[45] But while, like Green, Arnold rejected
the selfishness implied in traditional conceptions of liberty, he
did not take his alternative to the self-denying lengths of Green.
As Melvin Richter has argued, there was a marked æsceticism
about Green's ideal of freedom – enjoining self-sacrifice for the
sake of the common good to an extreme degree. That there was
any conflict between self-interest and the common good of
society was inconceivable to him. It was a conception of
freedom which enabled him to sanction a good deal of state
interference. This included restrictions upon the sale of liquor
and freedom of contract, the regulation of working conditions,
abolition of primogeniture whereby land remained concentrated
in the hands of a few great landowners, and the further
enforcement of compulsory primary education. Green believed
that the state, in acting thus, would enhance the powers of
individuals to contribute to the common good, helping to create
a society of sober, educated citizens, together with 'that
mainstay of social order and contentment – a class of small
proprietors tilling their own land' (125). Legislation in the
directions mentioned above would remove hindrances to
freedom in the positive sense in which Green had defined it.
Yet while he was not far from Mill in sanctioning a more than
minimal role for the state in these ways, Green attempted to do
so on principled, but ultimately vague, rather than pragmatic
grounds.[46] Moreover, his acceptance of the principles of private

---

[45] M. Arnold, *Culture and Anarchy: and other writings*, ed. S. Collini
(Cambridge, 1993). On Arnold's social and political theory see S. Collini,
Matthew Arnold: a critical portrait (Oxford: Clarendon Press, 1994).

[46] Greenleaf stresses that Mill made many qualifications to his principle of
'non-interference' by the state. He accepted 'a notable degree of government

property and freedom of contract were heavily qualified. Consequently, he introduced deep strains within the tradition of radical liberalism which he sought to uphold and strengthen.

The primacy which Green gave to an assumed common interest of society lay at the heart of this problem. Restrictions upon freedom of contract in the realms of housing and employment were necessary, he maintained, because the two parties occupied unequal positions. Employers and landlords thus had to comply with certain conditions in hiring labour (limiting the number of hours at work, protecting health, and so forth) and letting property, for otherwise employees and tenants would be treated as mere commodities. This defeated the end for which freedom of contract was the means: that is, 'the liberation of the powers of all men equally for contribution to a common good'. In the same way that employers and landlords were required to comply with certain health and safety measures, so private property was only warranted in so far as it facilitated 'that equal development of the faculties of all which is the highest good for all' (119).

It is difficult to square the priority which Green gave to an ideal of the social good as the justification for liberal institutions with their more conventional underpinning. Certainly, within traditional liberalism, freedom appears as an end in itself; by contrast, in Green's view, freedom is valuable merely as a means to the end of an ethic of public service. It is at this point that Green's place in the liberal tradition becomes anomalous. Anxious though he was that people's moral energies should not be impeded by the protection afforded by the state, he left little leeway as to the direction of those energies once liberated from the harsh conditions of a pure régime of freedom of contract. Aware – as had been a long line of Christian philosophers, from Aquinas through Locke – that the state was incapable of influencing internal motives, he cautioned against too extensive a role for the state. The function of the state was not to enforce moral goodness directly for this was an impossible task. Rather, it should provide the conditions in which true freedom – moral freedom – was

action that in fact amounts to a very formidable agenda indeed', Greenleaf, *op. cit.*, pp. 112–13.

possible. Still, his conception of true freedom was sharply and narrowly defined, and its scope circumscribed accordingly.

Herbert Spencer and the Bureaucratic State

Of all the thinkers included in this volume, Herbert Spencer (1820–1903) seems most loyal to the heritage of mid-Victorian radicalism, sustaining its crusade against a state based upon privilege and protectionism until the end of the nineteenth century. This loyalty is unsurprising, given Spencer's deep roots in the Nonconformist, industrial culture from which liberal radicalism had emerged. Born in Derby, Spencer's early life was dominated by the vigorous Dissenting beliefs of his father's family, in particular, who had dissented from the Wesleyan form of dissent to which his mother remained faithful. The extreme degree of his Nonconformity in all matters, religious, political, and social, is best illustrated in an early article he wrote for the *Westminister Review* in 1854, entitled 'On Manners and Fashions'. Castigating the power of convention in the form of deference to superiors, on the one hand, and dress codes, on the other, Spencer called for 'a protestantism in social usages'. The dead customs of etiquette which tyrannised the private lives of individuals were no more necessary to mankind than as the 'envelopes' in which government and despotic creeds flourished. Once a higher humanity had evolved, the protective shell of formality, in all its manifestations, could be cast off, and with that, government and organised religion too. 'Justice, kindness and beauty' would remain as the sole arbiters in mankind's dealings with each other.[47]

As a young man, in the early 1840s, Spencer became active in the Complete Suffrage Union, a middle class organization which took up the Chartists' campaign for a wide extension of the suffrage while dropping some of their more minor aims. Late in life, Spencer wrote in his *Autobiography* that the democratic opinions which he had supported in his youth were

---

[47] H. Spencer, 'On Manners and Fashions', *Essays on Education and Kindred Subjects* (London: J. M. Dent, 1911), pp. 234, 238.

regarded at the time as revolutionary. By the 1890s, he readily agreed with the apprehension which informed this judgement:

> for the drift towards Socialism, now becoming irresistible, has resulted from giving to the masses not a due proportion of power but the supreme power.[48]

Spencer had by no means turned against the radical principles of his youth in making this remark; on the contrary, he had seen fit in the intervening period to revise his hitherto optimistic theory of evolution in the light of social and political developments. In the 1840s and 1850s he had considered existing British society as poised at the threshold of a new era of industrialism, signalling the liberation of individuals through the supremacy of personal rights; whereas in the previous phase of militancy, now in its death-throes, the social bond was tightly sealed by status, coercion, and war. This confidence underlay the radical thrust of Spencer's *Social Statics* (1850), a work which proclaimed the law of equal freedom as the supreme moral end towards which humanity was steadily progressing. It also set out the social and political framework – including land nationalization, a call which Spencer was later to reject – in which the possibilities of mankind's perfect state would be maximized.

By the closing decades of the nineteenth century, Spencer was less certain that the progressive course of evolutionary change that he had earlier marked out was inexorable. Writing in the full flush of the middle-class victory over the landed classes in the 1850s and 1860s, he had failed to forsee the re-emergence of old forms of coercion with the rise to political power of the working class. As he explained the alteration of his political views brought about by this perception in his *Autobiography*,

> the temporary freedom obtained by abolishing one class of restraints, which reached its climax about the middle of the century, has since been decreased by the rise of another class of restraints, and will presently be no greater than it was before... [F]or in our day, as in past days,

---

[48] H. Spencer, *An Autobiography*, 2 vols., I (London: Williams & Norgate, 1904), pp. 220–21.

there co-exist the readiness to coerce and the readiness to submit to coercion... Whereas, in the days of early enthusiasm, I thought that all would go well if governmental arrangements were transformed, I now think that transformations in governmental arrangements can be of use only in so far as they express the transformed nature of citizens.[49]

In the growth of state interference at the end of the nineteenth century, Spencer perceived the revival of militancy in the new guise of socialism – the theme of his polemical work of 1884, *The Man Versus the State*. Strengthened by the misplaced altruism of much current liberal opinion, socialism threatened to annul all the political reforms of the mid nineteenth century, returning mankind to the dark days of political serfdom and Toryism. Inspired by the unfounded belief that there should be no suffering in society, and that that which existed was society's own fault, socialism, together with its liberal derivatives, had set the state to work in ending all misery.[50] Without the movement towards democracy, however, socialism would have been halted in its tracks. Democracy, Spencer now saw at the end of the century, had become the 'great political superstition of the time', replacing the worn-out notion of the divine right of kings with the new but equally reprehensible idea of the 'divine right of the parliaments'.[51] Once it had been used successfully to eject the old ruling class, democracy became the mechanism for the installation of a new ruling class – the people themselves. What reason did Spencer give, as he surveyed the disaster of 'over-legislation' brought about by popular rule, for the swift evolutionary backtracking that had taken place?

In Spencer's answer to this question lies the essence of what M. W. Taylor has termed his 'modification' of the liberal radicalism of the middle of the century, effectively turning the latter into a 'defensive creed'.[52] It was a response that was

---

[49] *Ibid.* II, p. 466.
[50] H. Spencer, 'The Man Versus the State' (1884), in *Political Writings*, ed. J. Offer (Cambridge University Press, 1994), p. 81.
[51] *Ibid.*, p. 140.
[52] M. W. Taylor, *Men Versus the State: Herbert Spencer and late Victorian radicalism* (Oxford: Clarendon Press, 1992), p. 4.

steeped in his experience of the workings of democracy, a form of government which had proved merely a replacement of feudal by socialist despotism. The movement towards freedom, as he intimated in the quotation from his *Autobiography* cited above, had been arrested by human nature itself – individuals had proved unable to accept the exacting responsibilities that accompany personal freedom.

Spencer elaborated upon this argument in the essay of 1891 reprinted here. The piece appeared in a volume of essays written by political thinkers and politicians who were much in sympathy with Spencer's concern at the collectivist course which British politics was currently taking. Indeed, the co-writers were more radical then Spencer himself, their views bordering on anarchism, a situation which greatly alarmed Spencer, painfully aware as he was that social arrangements could not run ahead of human nature.[53] The title of his essay – 'From Freedom to Bondage' – well suggests the reverse which Spencer believed that the cause of liberty had suffered of late. His explanation was the restlessness which men feel when any one position has been occupied for some length of time. As with an easy chair which one grows tired of after a while, exchanging it for a hard chair 'previously occupied and rejected', so humanity had grown dissatisfied with the new régime that had replaced the old. They had grown impatient with the era of freedom, 'easy' though it was, because of the new stresses and pains it imposed. Instead of settling down to a strenuous but beneficial process of spontaneous adaptation, 'incorporated humanity' had shown its desire to 'try another system'. This other system – namely socialism – 'is, in principle if not in appearance, the same as that which during past generations was escaped from with much rejoicing' (143).

Thus industrialism, or the régime of contract, had been short-lived, the régime of status being hastily reinstated when its successor proved too onerous to sustain in the short-term.

---

[53] R. Barker, *Political Ideas in Modern Britain: in and after the twentieth century* (1978; 2nd ed. London: Methuen, 1997), p. 63. On the reception of Spencer's later political thought see M. W. Taylor (ed.), *Herbert Spencer and the Limits of the State: the late 19th-century debate between individualism and collectivism* (Bristol: Thoemmes Press, 1996).

Spencer by no means denied the misery which existed in a society held together by voluntary co-operation through the precarious bonds of contract. His 1891 essay indicates the extent of his awareness of the evils of the 'struggle for existence' in a society organized around free contract. Those he enumerated included lying, dishonesty, bribery and fraud, cheap and shoddy goods, disproportionate reward of the workers relative to the organisers of industry. Moreover,

> The strong divisions of rank and the immense inequalities of means, are at variance with that ideal of human relations on which the sympathetic imagination likes to dwell; and the average conduct, under the pressure and excitement of social life as at present carried on, is in sundry respects repulsive. (137–8)

However, Spencer could not believe that these evils of industrialism outweighed the enormous benefits it had also yielded. The benefits were the same for Spencer as they had been for Adam Smith, and were extolled with all of the latter's awe and pride. The system based upon demand and supply,

> and the desire of each man to gain a living by supplying the needs of his fellows, spontaneously evolve that wonderful system whereby a great city has its food daily brought round to all doors or stored at adjacent shops; has clothing for its citizens everywhere at hand in multitudinous varieties; has its houses and furniture and fuel ready made or stocked in each locality; and has mental pabulum from halfpenny papers, hourly hawked round, to weekly shoals of novels, and less abundant books of instruction, furnished without stint for small payments. (148–9)

The system of voluntary co-operation in industry and society was made all the more appealing to Spencer when contrasted with the only alternative: compulsory co-operation enforced by public officials. His deep aversion to the latter constituted the *leit motif* of his liberalism. The basis of his antipathy was two-fold. First, state officialdom was inherently incapable of meeting society's needs with anything like the same efficiency as the system of contract and competition. Short of the existence of 'vast administrations', it was inconceivable that officials could accomplish what private traders could accomplish in providing the commodities needed to sustain urban life, let alone in organizing agriculture, commerce, power, transport, and industry on a much wider basis. But leaving aside the issue of efficient organization, there was the second problem of the threat to liberty posed by regulative agencies of all kinds, not just those belonging to the state. The tendency of regulative structures to become all powerful within their own organizations was inevitable; therefore, the agencies themselves must be kept to a minimum. Learned societies, trade unions, joint-stock companies alike, all tended to be driven by executive boards, often against the resistance of their members. But at least in existing society, they were kept under the restraint of law and subject to 'the criticisms and reprobations of an independent press' (154).

In this argument, Spencer revealed the same distrust of organizations and their threat to individual liberty as Dicey. But his imagination was far more fertile in predicting, on current trends, the development of a social system of the future in which industry after industry and function after function had become organized by the state. To the retort that such a vision was fanciful, Spencer argued that fifty years previously it would have been inconceivable that the grant in aid of compulsory education would rise three-fold and more, accompanied by grants for food and clothing too. He continued:

> No one, I say, would have dreamt that out of so innocent-looking a germ would have so quickly evolved this tyrannical system, tamely submitted to by people who fancy themselves free. (148)

Unchecked, there would quickly emerge a 'vast army of officials', gradually intermarrying with like grades, creating a caste with a common sense of superiority over the only other class in society – the 'regulated class'. Finally – and here Spencer addressed those liberals who seemed to have deserted the old cause of political for social reform – history would come full circle: for eventually, there would emerge 'a new aristocracy far more elaborate and better organised than the old' (150). Under a contractual régime of society, a dissatisfied worker could offer his labour elsewhere; under the military régime of socialism, 'he cannot be accepted elsewhere, save by order of the authorities' (144).

It was a spectre that Spencer intended to appear far more chilling than his own prescription for dealing with the ills that were inevitably suffered in the transitional period between the old, coercive and the new, contractual social order – that is, an unmitigated 'struggle for survival'. Implicitly, in the radical writings of his youth, Spencer had underestimated the capacity of human nature to adapt to the new social conditions. The emphasis of his later writings was on the necessity of much suffering and misery as human beings underwent the painful process of harmonizing their constitution with a greatly altered set of circumstances. Until recently, humanity had more or less existed in the 'savage state', only slowly emerging from a condition in which 'small numbers supported themselves on wild food'. It now had to adapt to 'the civilized state in which the food required for supporting great numbers can be got only by continuous labour' (155). To Spencer at the end of the nineteenth century, the perfection signified by the law of equal freedom – with the state ensuring national defence, public order, and personal safety only – seemed far more distant than in the heyday of liberal radicalism. All he could do was to place his trust in the discipline of the new order of society eventually being allowed to run its course. This would stimulate the conscious effort by which individuals would adopt the character necessary for a life of freedom. At present, Spencer gloomily concluded, the sense of justice 'which at once insists on personal freedom and is solicitous for the like freedom of others...exists but...very inadequate[ly]...' (156).

Conclusion

From the 1860s onwards, it is clear that British liberalism sustained the sharp, critical edge which had provided its earlier momentum and had led to the triumphs of 1846 and 1867. Significantly, however, liberal thinkers beyond this mid-Victorian apogee began to bring their own tradition rather than the national character and history more widely into question. In retrospect, the Repeal of the Corn Laws and the Second Reform Act seemed, at best, merely limited and partial instalments of the liberal ideal. Subsequent liberal thinkers attributed the shortcomings of mid-Victorian liberalism to a want of appreciation – not least among liberals – of those aspects of a general English tradition which were permeated with liberal values. The Liberalism and the notion of a coherent and elevated national past were thus eminently compatible, not at loggerheads as radical liberals had previously presumed. This movement within liberalism culminated in a much keener emphasis upon national unity towards the end of the century, a theme well illustrated in the liberal historiography of S. R. Gardiner which played down the searing religious differences of seventeenth-century Britain.[54] It also provided some of the core images of the enhanced sense of 'Englishness' which prevailed after the First World War.[55]

This strong patriotic vein in post-1860s liberalism forms an unstated assumption in all the essays which are reprinted in this book. It was more fully articulated in the larger works of their authors, indicating a positive attitude towards historical aspects of Englishness that had tended to be absent in the thought of their immediate liberal predecessors. It is certainly significant that three out of four of the authors who were still alive in 1886 – Stephen, Dicey, and Spencer – supported Liberal Unionism in the crisis within the Liberal party over Irish Home Rule. This was a touchstone of English identity, if not of liberalism generally. A fourth author – Acton – accepted Home Rule, but only reluctantly. For Acton, the most that could be said for it was that it was 'necessary, dangerous, unhopeful', pessimism which he shared with his friend and fellow liberal, James Bryce.[56]

Stephen's patriotism lies most obviously at the root of his liberalism, as we have seen. It is well illustrated in his article

---

[54]   T. Lang, *The Victorians and the Stuart Heritage: interpretations of a discordant past* (Cambridge University Press, 1995), p. 167.

[55]   For one interpretation of how the First World War heightened English national identity – and brought images of the English character such as Stephen's into wide circulation – see J. M. Winter, 'British National Identity and the First World War' in S. J. D. Green and R. C. Whiting (eds.), *The Boundaries of the State in Modern Britain* (Cambridge University Press, 1996).

[56]   See H. A. L. Fisher, *James Bryce*, 2 vols., I (London: MacMillan, 1927), p. 196. I am most grateful to Professor Christopher Harvie for this point.

on 'Liberalism' and further, in his attack upon Mill in *Liberty, Equality, Fraternity*. For example, he there argued that Mill's folly, in pleading for tolerance in society, was to ignore the very real and eternal conflict that always exists in questions of morals and religion. Such matters could not be left unsettled. Far better than demanding tolerance in the form of indifference was to encourage the conduct of disputes in a spirit of fairness, humanity, goodwill, and temperance – in short, a liberal spirit. These qualities, maintained Stephen, produced a courageous, noble character that was 'a peculiar merit of English people'. He continued:

> Every event of our lives, from schoolboy games up to the most important struggles of public life, even, as was shown in the 17th [*sic.*] century, if they go the length of civil war, is a struggle in which it is considered a duty to do your best to win, to treat your opponents fairly, and to abide by the result in good faith when you lose, without resigning the hope of better luck next time.[57]

War and defeat were unavoidable. Still, 'we can fight according to our national practice like men of honour and people who are friends at bottom, and without attaching an exaggerated value to the subject matter of our contention.'[58]

The loyalty of Acton and Dicey to English political institutions has also been emphasized in this introduction. While Acton became ambivalent towards the features he had once praised in connection with Englishness – tolerance, diversity, tradition – nonetheless he elicited the admiration of liberals subsequently, on the basis of his earlier attitudes.[59] The locus of Dicey's national pride in the Common Law tradition as the foundation of English liberty and individualism sets him apart from many mid-Victorian liberals, for whom the national past held few, if any redeeming features. His denial of sharp class distinctions in English society in his essay 'The Balance of Classes' is also symptomatic of a more emollient form of liberalism.

---

[57] J. F. Stephen, *Liberty, Equality, Fraternity*, p. 149.
[58] J. F. Stephen, *op. cit.*, pp. 149–50.
[59] Two such liberals were Ernest Barker (1874–1960) and F. A. Hayek (1899–1992).

T. H. Green's adherence to an ideal of liberty that was rooted in England's past as much as in its future is most evident in his 'Four Lectures on the English Revolution' (1867).[60] It was from the Independents in the English Civil War, notably Sir Henry Vane, that Green derived his ideal of religious citizenship – that is, service to the common good. There are also strong Burkean overtones to his liberalism in presuming a sense of national identity as the basis of a citizen's attachment to the state. Consciousness of a 'common dwelling place' with its history and traditions was essential to the conversion of mere obedient citizens into 'loyal subjects' and even 'intelligent patriots'.[61]

Finally, Herbert Spencer too invoked a conception of the distinctiveness and superiority of English national character in certain respects in arguing for liberalism. His dismay at the increasing interventionist character of the British state in the 1880s and 1890s must have been heightened by a belief that the relaxation of the rigour of militancy in Europe was, until that point, especially advanced 'in our own country' (142). The same pride in English progress away from a régime of 'compulsory co-operation' can be found in Spencer's early works, for example, his *Social Statics*.[62] The reader is there asked to compare 'English energy and continental helplessness'. Spencer then gave a catalogue of English achievements abroad, including the first gas works in Paris, 'after the failure of a French company', and 'many of the gas-works throughout Europe'; steam navigation on the Rhone and the Danube, 'after the French and Germans had failed'; the great suspension bridge at Pesth and a 'still greater suspension bridge' over the Dnieper; and so on. Naturally, Spencer identified English virtues with the mechanical arts and entrepreneurship. These achievements were, in turn, closely

---

[60]   T. H. Green, 'Four Lectures on the English Revolution', in R. L. Nettleship (ed.), *The Works of Thomas Hill Green*, 3 vols., III (London: Longmans, 1889).

[61]   On Green's patriotism, and that in English Idealism more generally, see J. Stapleton, *Englishness and the Study of Politics: the social and political thought of Ernest Barker* (Cambridge University Press, 1994), chap. 1.

[62]   H. Spencer, *Social Statics: or the conditions essential to human happiness specified, and the first of them developed* (London: Watts & Co., 1850).

associated with the 'discipline' imposed by the industrial type of society he was so concerned to vindicate and which was of comparatively recent origin. But although antiquity was hardly the essence of the English tradition to which Spencer was so endeared, the underlying qualities of character as he perceived them were more deeply rooted in the peculiar form which government – and implicitly 'militant' aristocratic government – had taken in Britain. He wrote:

> Having been left in a greater degree than others to manage their own affairs, the English people have become self-helping, and have acquired a great practical ability. Whilst conversely that comparative helplessness of the paternally-governed nations of Europe...is a natural result of the state-superintendence policy – is the reaction attendant on the action of official mechanisms...[63]

As a consequence, the English had enjoyed a considerable advantage over their continental neighbours in the movement towards industrialism, despite an early lack of manufacturing expertise.

Spencer's unconscious tribute to the legacy of aristocratic government in England points forward to a significant change in liberal attitudes towards the past. No longer demanding a fresh start, a broader range of liberal thinkers after 1860 were inclined to seek the sanction of tradition for the standards and ideals by which the future should be shaped.

The post-1860 alliance between liberal England and historic Englishness terminated only with the sharp decline of both ideals after the Second World War. Its passing came with the triumph of social democracy in the form of state planning and welfare. While usually interpreted as essentially a polemic against socialism, F. A. Hayek's *The Road to Serfdom* (1944) was equally an epitaph for late-Victorian English liberalism in which freedom ranked as both a supreme moral good and the cornerstone of a much cherished national inheritance. Writing on the difference of political outlook in Britain during the First World War, as compared with the Second, Hayek maintained:

---

[63]   *Ibid.*, pp. 392–3.

It is scarcely an exaggeration to say that the more typically English a writer on political or social problems then appeared to the world, the more is he to-day forgotten in his own country. Men like Lord Morley or Henry Sidgwick, Lord Acton or A. V. Dicey, who were then admired in the world at large as outstanding examples of the political wisdom of liberal England, are to the present generation largely obsolete Victorians.[64]

[64]   F. A. Hayek, *The Road to Serfdom* (1944; London: Routledge, 1991), p. 136.

BIBLIOGRAPHY

Primary reading

Arnold, M., *Culture and Anarchy: and other writings*, ed. S. Collini (Cambridge University Press, 1993).

Bright, J., *Selected Speeches of the Rt.Honble. John Bright M. P. on Public Questions* (London: J. M. Dent, 1907).

Dicey, A. V., *Lectures on the Relation between Law and Public Opinion in England during the Nineteenth Century* (1905; 2nd ed. London: Macmillan, 1940).

——————, 'The Combination Laws as Illustrating the Relation between Law and Opinion in England during the Nineteenth Century', *Harvard Law Review* 17 (1904), pp. 511–32.

——————, 'The Parliament Act, 1911, and the Destruction of all Constitutional Safeguards', in Sir William Anson et al., *Rights of Citizenship: a survey of safeguards for the people* (London: Frederick Warne, 1912).

——————, *Introduction to the Study of the Law of the Constitution,* 10th ed. (1885; London: Macmillan, 1962).

Essays on Reform (London: Macmillan, 1867).

Green, T. H., *Lectures on the Principles of Political Obligation and other Writings*, ed. P. Harris and J. Morrow (Cambridge University Press, 1986).

——————, 'Four Lectures on the English Revolution', in R. L. Nettleship (ed.), *The Works of Thomas Hill Green*, III (London: Longmans, 1889).

Hayek, F. A., *The Road to Serfdom* (1944; reprinted London: Routledge, 1991).

Hutton, R. H., *Criticisms on Contemporary Thought and Thinkers: selected from The Spectator*, 2 vols., vol. 1 (London: Macmillan, 1894).

Mill, J. S., 'The Spirit of the Age, 3' [Part 2], *The Examiner,* 13 March 1831, in *Collected Works of John Stuart Mill* 22 (Toronto: University of Toronto, 1986).

————, 'Recent Writers on Reform', *Fraser's Magazine* (April 1859), in *Dissertations and Discussions: political, philosophical and historical,* 2nd ed. (London: Longmans, 1875).

————, *On Liberty,* ed. S. Collini (Cambridge University Press, 1989).

Paul, H., ed., *Letters of Lord Acton to Mary, daughter of the Right. Hon. W.E. Gladstone* (London: George Allen, 1904).

Pyle, A. (ed.), *Liberty: contemporary responses to John Stuart Mill* (Bristol: Thoemmes Press, 1994).

Questions for a Reformed Parliament (London: Macmillan, 1867).

Spencer, H., 'On Manners and Fashions', in *Essays on Education and Kindred Subjects* (London: J. M. Dent, 1911).

————, *An Autobiography,* 2 vols. (London: Watts & Co., 1904).

————, 'The Man Versus the State' (1884), in *Political Writings,* ed. J. Offer (Cambridge University Press, 1994).

————, *Social Statics: or the conditions essential to human happiness specified, and the first of them developed* (1850; London: Watts & Co., 1910).

Stephen, James Fitzjames, *Liberty, Equality, Fraternity: and three brief essays* (1873; reprinted University of Chicago Press, 1991).

Taylor, M. W. *Herbert Spencer and the Limits of the State: the late 19th-century debate between individualism and collectivism* (Bristol: Thoemmes, 1996).

Secondary reading

Barker, R., *Political Ideas in Modern Britain: in and after the twentieth century* (1978; 2nd ed., London: Methuen, 1997).

Burgess, M., *The British Tradition of Federalism* (London: Leciester University Press, 1995).

Burns, J. H., 'J. S. Mill and Democracy, 1829–1861', in J. B. Schneewind (ed.), *Mill: a collection of critical essays* (London: Macmillan, 1968).

Collini, S., *Public Moralists: political thought and intellectual life in Britain, 1850–1930* (Oxford: Clarendon Press, 1991).

——————, *Matthew Arnold: a critical portrait* (Oxford: Clarendon Press, 1994).

Collini, S., Winch, D. and Burrow, J., *That Noble Science of Politics: a study in nineteenth-century intellectual history* (Cambridge University Press, 1983).

Fisher, H. A. L., *James Bryce*, 2 vols. (London: MacMillan, 1927).

Francis, M. and Morrow, J., *A History of English Political Thought in the Nineteenth Century* (New York: St Martin's Press, 1994).

Grainger, J. H., *Character and Style in English Politics* (Cambridge University Press, 1969).

——————, *Patriotisms: Britain 1900–1939* (London: Routledge and Kegan Paul, 1986).

Greenleaf, W. H., *The British Political Tradition*, 3 vols., vol. 2, *The Ideological Heritage* (1983; London: Routledge, 1988).

Harvie, C., *The Lights of Liberalism: university liberals and the challenge of democracy, 1860–86* (London: Allen Lane, 1976).

Himmelfarb, G., *Victorian Minds* (London: Weidenfeld & Nicolson, 1968).

Lang, T., *The Victorians and the Stuart Heritage: interpretations of a discordant past* (Cambridge University Press, 1995).

Lippincott, B. E., *Victorian Critics of Democracy: Carlyle, Ruskin, Arnold, Stephen, Maine, Lecky* (Minneapolis: University of Minnesota Press, 1938).

Mathew, D., *Acton: the Formative Years* (London: Eyre & Spottiswode, 1946).

Meadowcroft, J., *Conceptualizing the State: innovation and dispute in British political thought 1880–1914* (Oxford: Clarendon Press, 1995).

Richter, M., *The Politics of Conscience: T. H. Green and his age* (London: Weidenfeld & Nicolson, 1964).

Roach, J., 'Liberalism and the Victorian Intelligentsia' (1957), in P. Stansky (ed.), *The Victorian Revolution: government and society in Victoria's Britain* (New York: New Viewpoints/Franklin Watts, 1973).

Smith, D., 'Englishness and the Liberal Inheritance after 1886', in R. Colls and P. Dodd (eds.), *Englishness: Politics and Culture 1880–1920* (Beckenham: Croom Helm, 1986).

Smith, K. J. M., *James Fitzjames Stephen: portrait of a Victorian rationalist* (Cambridge University Press, 1988).

Stapleton, J., *Englishness and the Study of Politics: the social and political thought of Ernest Barker* (Cambridge University Press, 1994).

————, 'Dicey and his Legacy', *History of Political Thought* 16, vol. 2 (1995), pp. 234–56.

Stephen, Leslie, *The Life of Sir James Fitzjames Stephen* (London: Smith, Elder & Co., 1895).

Sugarman, D., 'The Legal Boundaries of Liberty: Dicey, Liberalism and Legal Science', *The Modern Law Review* 46 (1983), pp. 102–11.

Taylor, M. W. *Men Versus the State: Herbert Spencer and late Victorian Radicalism* (Oxford: Clarendon Press, 1992).

Tulloch, H., *Acton* (London: Weidenfeld & Nicolson, 1988).

——————, *James Bryce's 'American Commonwealth': the Anglo-American background* (Woodbridge: Boydell Press, 1988).

Vincent, A. and Plant, R., *Philosophy, Politics, and Citizenship: the life and thought of the British Idealists* (Oxford: Blackwell, 1984).

Vincent, J., *The Formation of the British Liberal Party, 1857–1868* (1966; Harmondsworth: Penguin, 1972).

Viroli, M., *For Love of Country: an essay on patriotism and nationalism* (Oxford: Clarendon Press, 1995).

Winter, J. M., 'British National Identity and the First World War' in S. J. D. Green and R. C. Whiting (eds.), *The Boundaries of the State in Modern Britain* (Cambridge University Press, 1996).

LIBERALISM
JAMES FITZJAMES STEPHEN[*]

In all departments of life, abstract words play a most important
part, and there are some pursuits in which the great mass of
mankind never carry their inquiries further than is necessary to
ascertain which of two or three party catchwords are on the
whole most in harmony with the prevailing tone of their own
minds. This is true of politics beyond all other subjects. A good
party name saves all further trouble about the position of those
to whom it applies. The broad differences between extreme
political parties are always sufficiently well marked to admit of
no mistake, and emphatic nicknames provide a rough and
convenient classification to which all minor differences may be
referred. The best party names are those which are absolutely
unmeaning. The Montagne[a] and the Gironde,[b] in the French
Revolution, were admirable in their way, and the Right, Left,
and Centre of the constitutional period would have been equally
good if they had not been deficient in that slight touch of
grotesqueness which every durable nickname requires; the

---

[*] James Fitzjames Stephen, 'Liberalism', *The Cornhill Magazine*, V (1862),
pp. 70–84.

[a] Montagne. Name given to the extremist wing in the French Convention.
The radical policies of the Montagnards were influential from late 1792
until 1794.

[b] Gironde. Group of Deputies who were attacked by the Montagne. They
supported a vigorous war policy in the French Legislative Assembly but
became more moderate in the Convention.

Hunkers,[c] Barnburners,[d] and Know-nothings[e] of American politics, on the other hand, have it in excess, and are vulgar. On the whole, our own Whigs and Tories, perhaps, come as near to perfection as that human frailty which taints nicknames as well as other things will permit.

The party names which aim not merely at identifying political parties, but at describing their principles, require more attention. Something may almost always be learnt from them; though it is generally something different from that which entered into the minds of those who brought them into fashion. For example, a curious history attaches to the use of the words 'Republican' and 'Democratic', as expressing a contrast in American politics; and the same is true in a higher degree of the words Liberal, Radical, Conservative, and their strange compounds Liberal-Conservative and Conservative-Liberal, which are so constantly in use amongst us at the present day. To discuss party politics would be foreign to the purpose of this Magazine; but an inquiry into the general bearing of phrases which exercise so much influence over all our thoughts and much of our conduct, need not involve anything like political controversy.

The words 'liberal' and 'liberalism', like all other such phrases, derive a great part of their significance from the time when they were first invented. They came into general use on the Continent during the early part of the present century, and probably the first occasion in which they were brought conspicuously before Englishmen was when Lord Byron and his friends set up the periodical called the *Liberal* [f] to represent their views, not only in politics, but also in literature and religion. The *Liberal* met with little encouragement, and soon came to an end; but the same reasons which led to the adoption

---

[c] Hunkers, conservative group of New York Democrats in the 1840s. Violently opposed to antislavery agitation.

[d] Barnburners, radical group of New York Democrats (1844–54) and rival to the Hunkers. Clashed with the national party over slavery and many joined the Republicans in 1854. The Barnburners and Hunkers originated in canal politics.

[e] The Know-nothing Party, US political party of the 1850s, officially named the American Party in 1854. Formed as a reaction against Irish Catholic and German immigration.

[f] The *Liberal: verse and prose from the South*, by Leigh Hunt, Lord Byron and others, 1822, 1823.

of its title, gave the word wide currency both at home and abroad, and especially on the Continent. Like all other significant party names, it embodied a boast and a reproach. Those who originally adopted it as their title said in effect, 'The whole established order of things, political, literary, and religious, is narrow-minded and bigoted. We propose to reconstruct it upon larger and more generous principles; and, as the first step, we mean to break down what already exists.' It does not often happen that a title adopted by one party is accepted by their opponents, as an appropriate description of them, but it has been so in this case. The party whom the word Liberal was intended to taunt, admitted that it did describe their antagonists not unfairly, and attached to it some such interpretation as this:–'Yes, you are liberal; that is to say, you oppose yourselves to all the restraints which the imperfections of human nature require, and you have constructed in your own minds a romance about mankind which is completely gratuitous, but which you find to be indispensable to your licentious theories. You either leave out of sight all that is dark and bad in human nature, or you gild it with fine names, which it does not deserve; and this may well be called liberal; but it is the liberality of a moral spendthrift, who, having thrown to the winds his own principles, is willing to indulge every one else to the utmost in similar conduct.'

The equal and opposite injustice of these two interpretations of the same word expresses much of the essence of that silent struggle of feeling which, for several generations, and especially during the last two, has underlain the open controversies which have agitated politics, literature, and philosophy. There can be no doubt that both parties had much to say for themselves. There was plenty of bigotry on the one side, and plenty of licentiousness on the other; indeed, each was to be found in slightly different shapes on both sides, and the general result of the controversy cannot be said to have been favourable to either side exclusively. On the one hand, we have seen great alterations made in the form, and some alterations made in the spirit, of almost all the doctrines and institutions which were formerly in undisputed possession of our national belief and affections; but, on the other hand, those doctrines and institutions have, subject to these alterations, and to such others as may be agreed upon, been maintained, and in their modified form are as firmly and as widely rooted as ever. The deep changes which have been made in our institutions have made no one permanent and fundamental change in the sentiments or conduct of the nation. Nothing in the history of England is more striking than its continuity. Hardly at any time, never in modern times, has any one class of the community succeeded in getting the bit between its teeth, and riding roughshod over the sentiments and interests of the others.

The alternate and partial success of the two great parties which have struggled together so long, and with such qualified and intricate results, suggests the question what that moral principle is which gives them their strength, and what objects those who are animated by it would try to attain if they fully understood their own position, and were not biassed by temporary party objects. No doubt there are many such principles and objects, but some of them at least must be appropriately expressed by a word which has had so great a charm for a whole generation as 'liberalism', for it should be noticed that even those who tried to affix a reproachful meaning to it, usually admitted that its natural sense was eulogistic; indeed, they often stigmatized the views which they denounced as being infested with spurious liberalism, or as falsely claiming the title of liberal. There can, indeed, be no doubt that the word 'liberal' has a proper sense of its own, or that that sense is laudatory, for no one doubts it when it is applied to other than political purposes. It never could be doubted that to qualify a man's profession or education as 'liberal' was to pay him a compliment, and those who originally adopted the word as a party name meant, no doubt, to claim for their political opinions merits analogous to those which the common use of the word implies.

The meaning of the word, considered as denoting moral excellence, comes very near to that which the usage of our own day is gradually identifying with the word 'gentleman'. 'Gentleman' probably once denoted, as 'gentilhomme' does still, nothing more than the fact that a man belonged to one of a certain set of families. By degrees it came, as logicians say, to connote the assertion that he had also the moral and social qualities which a person so descended ought to have in order to justify the superiority which persons of rank habitually claim over their neighbours. In our own days, though the notion of some degree of rank – such an amount of it, at least, as raises the presumption of a good education – is still attached to the word 'gentleman', moral and social meanings connected with it are constantly assuming greater prominence, so that in course of time it may possibly come to be used simply as a term of moral approbation bearing no relation to the social rank of the persons to whom it is applied.

Should this ever be the case, it would coincide in part with the proper meaning of the word 'liberal'; but in part only, for 'gentleman' and 'gentlemanlike' imply nothing as to the intellectual powers of the persons to whom they are applied, whereas the word 'liberal' implies the possession of mental excellences cognate to the moral qualities which are its proper objects. If, therefore, the words 'liberal' and 'liberalism' were applied to political opinions and parties in their proper sense, they ought to denote, in the persons and parties signified, generous and high-minded sentiments upon political subjects, guided by a highly instructed, large-minded, and impartial intellect. Liberalism, in a word, ought to mean the opposite of sordidness, vulgarity, and bigotry. As generally used, however, 'liberal' and 'liberalism' are rather proper names than significant words, and denote in politics, and to some extent in literature and philosophy, the party which wishes to alter existing institutions with the view of increasing popular power. In short, they are not greatly remote in meaning from the words 'democracy' and 'democratic'. The historical reason of the connection between the two is, that those who first introduced the words in their present sense complained of the narrow-mindedness and bigotry of the state of things then existing, and proposed to introduce a higher conception of the ends and means of public life by an appeal to the people at large. To a great extent they have succeeded in attaining the means which they desired, and others have obtained it even more completely.

Popular power has increased vastly during the last half-century in our own country. In America and France it reigns without control, though under different forms; but the great political problem of the day – a problem infinitely more important than all party questions put together – is whether the second half of the hopes of the original liberals will be as widely fulfilled as the first; whether they will succeed not merely in increasing the power of the popular voice, but in raising thereby the general tone of public life, and in causing it to be pervaded by a higher conception of the objects of national existence. If they do succeed in this, they will have done a great thing; if they do not, they will have inflicted upon mankind the greatest of all curses – a permanent degradation of human life.

There are and may be endless controversies about forms of government and society; but one point is established almost beyond the reach of controversy. Once place the sovereign power unreservedly in the hands of the bulk of the community, and, whether they exercise it themselves, or delegate it to a single nominee, reform, by any process yet discovered, is at an end. This or that detail may be altered by discussion, but the general type of the national existence, the general objects and principles of its politics, are settled for ever. All political reforms spring from conflicts amongst the different parties, national or political, which constitute the body politic. Either the king calls in the people against the nobles; or the nobles ally themselves with the people against the king; or the people press the king and the nobles to give up a share of their joint power; or the clergy connects itself with one or more of the different constituent elements of the nation against the rest; and, as in every political struggle, each side is obliged to appeal to principles recognized by both, the result of such contests is often favourable to the whole nation. One party, for example, will seek to advance itself by its foreign policy, another by its advocacy of internal reforms, and so on. When, however, the bulk of the nation has, once for all, possessed itself of sovereign power, there is no more room for conflict and change than there is for currents and waterfalls, pools and eddies, when streams, whose channels cross, diverge and meet again on the mountain side, have united to form a calm, lowland river. A country which has reached the point of social and political equality will regulate its affairs according to the prevalent temper of the majority. The average mental level of the great mass will predominate with undisputed and indisputable force, and will fix the position and career of the nation as irresistibly as the social position of a middle-aged man, whose character is formed, is fixed by the general tone of his mind and the nature of his pursuits.

This being so, it is of the last importance that all who wish the triumph of liberalism to be a blessing and not a curse should endeavour by every means in their power to impress upon those whose political influence has been so much increased, the importance of the positive side of liberalism – that side which regards the end to be attained – a high and generous conception of national existence, and a policy to correspond with that conception. We have all been taught, almost to excess, that all the blood of all the Howards[g] cannot ennoble slaves, or fools, or cowards. It is far more important in our days to bear in mind that the truth is universal. A tinker or tailor may be as great a slave, fool, and coward as the heir of the proudest name in England; and if he is, votes and ballot-boxes will only degrade him further. If our labourers and mechanics are to legislate, their first need is to learn something of the spirit of legislators. If they are called, as they are often told, to rule a world, let them catch the imperial spirit. Whether our rulers are to bear the most famous or the humblest names, is of little moment; but whoever they are, let them, at least, be statesmen, scholars, and soldiers, fitted, as one of the greatest of Englishmen puts it, to discharge discreetly and magnanimously every office of war and peace.

It is possible and not uncommon to call upon the mass of the people to enter upon the government of the country in a different temper from this. There are those who point to the institutions of their country, and say to their hearers – You have at least broken the gates and scaled the walls of the stronghold of your enemies – of those who enslaved your fathers and oppressed yourselves – who, for their own vile and

---

[g] Possibly a reference to the Howard family beginning with Thomas Howard, third Duke of Norfolk and Earl of Surrey (1473–1554), brother-in-law of Henry VII; helped to defeat the Scots at Flodden Field (1513); uncle of both Anne Boleyn and Catherine Howard. His eldest son was executed by Henry VIII for treason. He himself was charged with treason by Henry VIII but was released by Queen Mary in 1553.

selfish objects, wasted your money and squandered your blood upon useless or criminal enterprises. Now enjoy the victory you have won; pull down the monuments of your disgrace, root up the institutions, destroy the sentiments, repeal the laws which were the work of the horde of tyrants who soon will be at your mercy, for are not their armaments and their offices mere nests of corruption? Are not their laws made on purpose to ensnare and to enslave? Would not their church persecute if it did not dote? Turn over a new leaf and open a new chapter in the history of England; renounce the criminal ambition which has borne such bitter fruit; prune away the institutions which trained the minds and consoled and guided the souls of the evil race on whom you have turned your backs; and having gratified your just indignation, live at ease amidst your mills and corn-fields, and let the England of the future look back upon the England of the past as on a bad dream which has passed away.

For many years past such exhortations have been put before Englishmen in various shapes. Popular speakers have addressed them in express words to crowded audiences; popular writers have insinuated them by the help of fiction, of irony, and of satire into the minds of audiences infinitely more numerous. It would be as invidious as it would be easy to specify books which have found their way to millions of readers, and which by their general temper and flavour, if not by their specific teaching, have preached such doctrines in their most seductive form – a form all the more seductive because it was indirect. The most careless reader of the endless books which in our days are written expressly for careless readers, cannot have failed to understand the sentimental sneer with which some of our most popular writers contrast the follies of men of rank with the virtues of impossible artisans; or the chuckle with which they illustrate by details, the impossibility of which neither they nor their readers have sufficient knowledge or patience to understand, the iniquities of the law and the corruption and blunders of the Government. Whatever form such doctrines may assume, their essence is the same. Whether, as may sometimes happen, they are elicited by genuine indignation against real abuses, or, as must often be the case, by envy, the vilest of all vices, they are suitable not for men who have any notion of freedom and self-respect, but

for slaves broken loose; and thus they are as insulting to those
to whom they are addressed as to those against whom they are
levelled.

The spirit in which a politician who deserved the title of
liberal would call upon the bulk of the population to take an
increased share in the government of the country would be the
reverse of this. He would look upon himself as a man charged
to introduce to his estate an heir who had attained his majority;
he would teach those whom he addressed to see in the
institutions of their native land neither a prison to escape from
nor a fortress to storm, but a stately and venerable mansion
which for eight centuries had been the home of their ancestors,
and in which they were now to take their place and play their
part. He would try to fix their attention, not on the petty side of
institutions, which little men can always think of in a petty
spirit, but on their dignified aspects; and he would show them
how that dignity was, in a vitally important sense, their own.

'You', he might say, 'are now to share the government of the
country with men whose ancestors have for centuries taken a
leading part in it and who owed their greatness to the fact, that
they inspired your ancestors with trust and confidence, and took
the lead in enterprises in which they eagerly followed. When
you see a man bearing a name which for centuries has been
illustrious in peace and war, and which is decorated by estates
and titles, you should regard him – not with the petulant envy
which hopes nothing, believes nothing, and endures nothing;
which thinks evil of every one, and rejoices in every man's
iniquities, because they are the garbage on which it is fed – but
with a generous and lawful pride, as one of the representatives
of that national greatness which is the common inheritance of
us all. The value of rank and titles is derived, not from their
intrinsic glitter, nor even from the old associations connected
with them, but from the fact that they designate their possessor
as one of the leading men in a great nation. Who honours a
Sicilian marquis or a Mexican field-marshal? An English title is
worth having, because it gives rank in England, and the value
of rank in England is derived from the greatness of the English
nation. A powerful and splendid aristocracy is to a nation what
his house and grounds, his picture gallery and library, are to a
nobleman. Magnificent and orderly splendour is one of the

rewards of ages of peace and concord, and one of the pledges of their continuance. To grudge its expense and to deny its utility is the part, not of liberality, but of stinginess.'

There is no point which a true liberal would be more anxious to impress upon the bulk of the population in connection with their accession to political power, than the vital importance of forming a lofty notion not merely of the splendour and of the history of their country, but of the part which it has to play in the world, and of the spirit in which it should play it. It is a difficult task to impress such views upon any body of men, and the difficulty increases in direct proportion to the ignorance and poverty of those who belong to it. An ignorant man cannot without great difficulty rise to anything like an adequate conception of the importance and permanence of the results of national policy. A poor man feels at once the sacrifices which such a policy often entails, and ignorance and poverty foster those petty, huxtering, narrow-minded views of both this world and the next, which are the greatest enemies of the policy which befits a great nation.

It has become a secondary commonplace to deny that a little knowledge is a dangerous thing, and to accumulate proofs of the not very surprising fact, that of the many meanings which may attach to a pungent saying, some are not true; but it is not only true, but most important, that to have inadequate views of great subjects is often a greater evil than to be completely ignorant of them. No sort of ignorance is so presumptuous, intolerant, and confident as the ignorance of all that lies outside of a trivial familiar range of thought. Hardly any night is so dark as to exclude the idea of space. Even if the moon and stars are not to be seen, and if the outlines of the landscape are blotted out, the clouds, the mist, and the indistinct forms of surrounding objects half perceived through the darkness, give a notion – sometimes a most powerful one – of vastness and grandeur; but a person sitting in a small room, well lighted by a single candle, and carefully protected by blinds and shutters, may be excused for forgetting for the moment that the world is more than ten feet square.

In the same way it is easy to produce a profound and even tremendous effect on a mass of completely ignorant people, by an appeal to their sympathies or imaginations. The audience

whom Peter the Hermit[h] stirred up to the crusades were as
ignorant as their impulses, on the whole, were noble; and much
of the enthusiasm of which the French Revolution was partly
the cause and partly the effect, was directed towards great and
not ignoble objects, though it was felt by the most ignorant
population in Europe, and though it was often abused by the
basest leaders to the vilest purposes. This sort of ignorance,
and this sort of enthusiasm, is not what in these days we have
to deal with. No one who really knows England or Englishmen
would seriously entertain the slightest hope or fear that the
policy of the country will ever be directed or even affected to
any considerable extent by passionate popular movements
directed towards large general objects. There is no chance here
and now either of a revolution or of a crusade. If we want to
see how the transfer of political power to the bulk of the
population would affect the general tone of the national policy,
we have only to look round us and to see what sort of topics
interest the class in question, and what is the manner in which
they like to see them handled. The evidence upon the subject is
ample. It may be collected from newspapers, from popular
magazines, from the experience of candidates at elections for
large places, from the open-air discussions upon politics,
theology, and other subjects which take place wherever
labouring men have a little leisure, open space, and moderately
fine weather. Any one who studies these various kinds of
evidence with anything like the attention which they deserve as
indications of the character of those who are often regarded as
the future rulers of this great nation, will be led to form
conclusions materially different from those which a very
influential class of popular writers suggest.

Formerly labourers, mechanics, and small shopkeepers were
represented by almost all writers, whether popular or
speculative, as ignorant and foolish in the highest degree, or, at
any rate, as quite incapable of having an opinion upon any but

[h]   Peter the Hermit (d.1115), French popular preacher who led thousands of
followers into the Balkans ahead of the knightly crusading armies of Urban
II. While his flock disgraced themselves in Christian territories, and were
shipped to Asia Minor by an apprehensive Byzantine government – where
most of them were massacred by Turks – Peter joined the main (first)
crusade.

the commonest affairs of life, and as requiring, even in reference to such affairs, the constant superintendence and advice of their social superiors. This view of the case was obviously unjust, and was succeeded by another which still has many influential partisans, though it is quite as untrue, and perhaps even more dangerous. For about twenty years past, the 'working man' has been the subject of a sort of apotheosis. Some of the most popular writers in the language delight to contrast his ardent thirst for knowledge, his grasp of facts, his rugged strength of character, his forcible language and expressive metaphors, with the tame and somewhat feeble propriety which is ascribed to persons in easy circumstances. The novels of Mr. Disraeli (who was one of the earliest promulgators of this theory), Mr. Dickens, Mr. Kingsley, Mrs. Gaskell, and those of almost every other writer whose works are much coloured by the notion of great impending political changes in which the bulk of the population are to play a conspicuous part, are filled with delineations of stern and somewhat terrible working men, who are always embodying profound observations in studiously bad grammar, and hinting that they have a knowledge of secrets and a control over powers which would frighten out of their propriety the actual possessors of political power, if they were but aware of them. So strong was the impression produced by these and other writers of the same sort, that ten years ago a young man fresh from college was heard, after an hour's conversation with a Manchester mill hand, to express his surprise that he could not conscientiously say that his acquaintance appeared to him superior to the average of the undergraduates to whom he had been accustomed.

If the young gentleman had continued his researches, his scepticism would probably have been largely increased. Any one who is accustomed to watch the way in which real mechanics and labourers talk, speak, and argue, and to observe the tone of the books and newspapers which they really like to read, will see that there is more difference, and a more durable difference, between minds which have and have not been formed by a liberal education than between the bodies of a sedentary invalid and a trained athlete. The general impression made on the mind of a person who knows what the conversation of men of really high instruction is like, by the arguments of a knot of intelligent mechanics upon politics or theology, is remarkable. It is, that he is talking to men who have never learned to use their minds, and who, if they had learned to think, have hardly any materials for thought. The subjects which attract their attention are almost always matters which have been left far behind by the general course of thought, and in politics especially are either trivial, or, if important, are treated in so narrow a way as to make the truth or falsehood of the conclusion ultimately reached almost entirely a matter of chance.

At a late contested election for one of the metropolitan boroughs, the question which really came home to the hearts of the electors was flogging in the army. What they really cared about – the observation on national affairs which it appeared to them essential to make – was, that flogging in the army was a bad thing. This supplies a good specimen of the way in which uneducated men must of necessity regard politics when they are not under the influence of temporary gregarious excitement. They have never had an opportunity of looking at anything whatever comprehensively. Their literary education, such as it is, is usually over, even in favourable cases, before they are engaged, with few exceptions, in learning and applying processes which, in themselves, have no tendency to develop any of the higher powers of the mind. A man, for example, is a carpenter, any by practice acquires a certain facility of eye and hand which enables him to guide his tools right, and to measure the quantity and direction of the effort to be made; but there is nothing in this which teaches him to classify, to distinguish, or to infer. Part of his leisure he passes in reading – principally the newspapers; but he has no occasion to labour at his reading, and he gets little more from it than a stock of ready-made sentiments and opinions, and a certain familiarity with language which is generally more pretentious than expressive. The real intelligent mechanic is not an uncouth Titan, struggling against Etnas which society has piled upon him, but a sturdy, ingenious, sensitive man, with little knowledge and narrow and slightly made opinions.

Such as they are, however, the opinions of a slightly educated man are opinions as well as any others, and the collective power and numerical importance of slightly educated people is so great, that they effectually keep each other in countenance, and conceal from each other's observation the fact that their education is slight, and that their views are narrow. Nor is this all. By degrees, the existence of so large and influential an audience attracts preachers and advocates suited to its capacity. Men are found to construct theories of all sorts adapted for its belief. Booksellers know well that there are several distinct literatures adapted to the wants of readers of different calibres. Some of the most popular novels that ever were written, novels sold by tens of thousands, are utterly destitute of all the literary qualities which any high or careful education would produce or require in an author. Sermons which find, perhaps, as many readers as the novels are absolute nonsense, full of blunders, which nothing but the grossest ignorance could commit or fail to detect. Newspapers are, by far, the best written part of the literature which circulates widely amongst artisans and mechanics, and they, from the nature of the ease, must always be written to be read in a few minutes, and forgotten as soon as they are read. By these and similar means, a curious result is, in course of time, produced. Slight plausible theories upon all sorts of subjects are invented and made to pass current amongst mankind with a strange facility. People get their minds filled with rather reasonable sophistry, which they do not, in the least degree, suspect to be sophistical. A set of secondary commonplaces (like that referred to above, about the benefits of a little knowledge) are made popular, and not only look like real opinions, but exercise as much weight over public affairs as if they were real, if not more.

A curious proof of this is to be found in the habitual language of newspaper writers, even the best of the number. They constantly appeal to what is eulogistically described as a 'healthy popular sentiment', a 'popular instinct', and rest the claims of statesmen to influence and office on the fact that they succeed in hitting the exact line which such sentiments or instincts approve. A good illustration of this was lately afforded by the most influential paper in England. In discussing the question whether or not clergymen ought to be allowed to preach certain doctrines which were admitted to be unusual, it became necessary to say something of the limits within which it was desirable to circumscribe their liberty. The limit laid down was neither truth, which might have occurred to some, nor orthodoxy, which might have occurred to others. It was simply this – that clergymen ought to publish nothing which they ought not to preach, and that they ought to preach nothing which could shock or startle ordinary fathers of families. It did not appear to occur to the writer that ordinary fathers of families might be very ignorant and narrow-minded, and might never have paid any attention to theology, or that it would make any difference whether or not this were so. His view was, that the use of the clergy was to preach the kind of matter which the congregation, rightly or not, liked to hear. If he went out of that circle, he might be a great philosopher, a sound divine, a good man; but he was not fit to be in charge of an English parish. The general sentiment of the congregation was to decide what was to be preached to it, and if that sentiment was in any respect blind or defective, it was to improve and enlarge itself; it was not the business of any constituted authority, ecclesiastical or civil, to enlarge or improve it.

It is in this danger of deifying almost casual public opinions and slight and ineffectual public sentiments that the danger of political liberalism lies; and it is just the danger to which it ought to be most deeply alive, and against which it ought to take the most careful precautions, if it is ever to redeem the pledge which its title implies. Those only are entitled to the description as well as to the name of liberals, who recognise the claims of thought and learning, and of those enlarged views of men and institutions which are derived from them, to a permanent preponderating influence in all the great affairs of life. The highest function which the great mass of mankind could ever be fitted to perform, if the highest dreams of the most enlightened philanthropists were fully realized, would be that of recognising the moral and intellectual superiority of the few who, in virtue of a happy combination of personal gifts with accidental advantages, ought to be regarded as their natural leaders, and of following their guidance, not slavishly but willingly, and with an intelligent co-operation. It is in the hands of such persons only that national affairs will be handled in a magnanimous and truly liberal temper, and that the vast wealth and power which ages of peace and plenty have stored up can be directed to adequate purposes.

Up to the present day minorities, which have generally been open to the influence of broad and high-minded views of the objects and character of national existence, notwithstanding faults which went far to counter-balance even that merit, have, with immense exceptions and interruptions, governed most of the great European nations. They were enabled to do so by institutions which are now almost universally broken down. Notwithstanding great baseness, much corruption, and infinite shortcomings of every kind, national affairs have, in modern Europe, been carried on on a magnificent scale and with glorious results. Institutions and the vestiges of them exist in every nation, and especially in our own, which still testify to the noble views and generous confidence of those who founded them, and which have proved by their history that those views were not unsound, and that that confidence was not altogether misplaced.

To take one instance amongst many, was not a firm belief in the notion that theological truth is both important and attainable, shown by the establishment of Christianity in a legal form and with proprietary rights in every nation of modern Europe? and was not the wish to guide the minds of men towards what was looked upon as the highest form of truth in itself liberal and noble? It is usually regarded, and possibly with justice, as a great discovery of modern wisdom, that governments have, as such, no religious character or duties whatever. This may be quite true; but if it is a truth, it is one which lowers our conception of the importance of governments, and diminishes our interest in their proceedings. One of the principal characteristics of our day is the facility with which people agree to differ upon every sort of subject, and the readiness with which a man's determination to enrol himself in any one of a considerable number of small coteries, social, political, or religious, is accepted as final by the rest of the world. It is, however, a consequence of the same temper that the pretension to stand aloof from all such coteries is regarded with dislike, and indirectly punished by a noiseless excommunication which gently extinguishes the influence of the man on whom it falls, and quietly shuts him out from all important communication with his neighbours, though it leaves his character and property untouched. This mode of treating all the greatest subjects of thought and feeling as private individual questions on which no public authority pronounces any opinion whatever has, no doubt, many conveniences; but it has also a strong tendency to narrow the minds of those who adopt it, and to give us all the air of dwarfs, living each in a separate corner of the house which our fathers built, and congratulating ourselves on the fact that we no longer find it necessary to quarrel as to who is to give orders, or how the rooms are to be arranged.

The great characteristic danger of our days is the growth of this quiet ignoble littleness of character and spirit. Unless liberals are able to do as much in the positive as they have done in the negative direction, they may come to be compared to a man who, seeing a high-spirited horse plunging and rearing and covered with sweat and foam, says to the rider, 'Remove the burden of your weight from that noble creature; take off the saddle which frets his back, and the cruel bit which galls his mouth, and you will see that, instead of wasting his strength in useless struggles, he will travel ten times as far and as fast as you can ride him.' If the rider hesitates to surrender his seat, the bystander is apt to cut his girths and bring him to the ground. But what becomes of the horse when his bit and bridle are gone? He does not get over more ground than before. He does not even prance and curvet, but, having kicked up his heels, shaken his head, and possibly rolled, he crops the grass by the roadside in contented ignorance of the hills and plains through which he would otherwise have passed.

We have not as yet gone far in the ignominious path which leads to national littleness, though the symptoms that we are in danger of entering on it are neither few nor unimportant, and require the most careful attention of those who have removed – not, certainly, before the time for their removal had arrived – many of the securities which we formerly possessed for a high-minded management of public affairs. They ought, therefore, now to set up as high a standard as can be raised of the powers and duties of the nation, and to diffuse a knowledge of it as widely as possible amongst those whom they have called into the national councils. It ought to be an elementary and universally acknowledged truth that the whole nation will be disgraced and stultified if the changes which have been and will be made in its constitution do not make our history even more glorious, our institutions more fruitful and venerable, our list of great names and great achievements richer, and our national character graver, stronger, and nobler than it has ever been before. It would be pedantic to affect to lay down rules as to the manner in which such great results could be brought about. Nations grow, like men, by exercise; and their function is, in the noble words already quoted, to discharge magnanimously and discreetly every office of peace and war. Many such offices court our attention, and we should do more to promote true liberalism by discharging them in a liberal imperial spirit than by any number of reform bills, though these, no doubt, have their uses.

By way of illustration, a single instance may be mentioned which is, perhaps, the most instructive of all. By a series of events hardly paralleled in the history of the world we have become the absolute masters of the Indian empire, with its 150,000,000 inhabitants. The whole fabric of that empire is a monument of energy, skill, and courage, and on the whole of justice and mercy, such as the world never saw before. How are we to deal with this great inheritance bequeathed to us by all that ought to touch us to the heart, by the courage of heroes, by the wisdom of statesmen, by victory and defeat, by the glories of Plassy [i] and Assaye,[j] by the agonies of Afghanistan[k] and Cawnpore? [l] Here, if anywhere, is an opportunity for true liberalism; here is an occasion where not to be great is to be

---

[i]   Plassey, place of Robert Clive's victory on 23 June 1757, which marked the birth of the British Indian empire.

[j]   Assaye, on 23 September 1803 the British, under General Arthur Wellesley, defeated the Sindhia dynasty of Gwalior, ending the Second Maratha war.

[k]   Afghanistan, the first Afghan war took place between 1838–42. British forces had invaded Afghanistan in 1838 to limit Russian influence. The Afghan uprising in October 1841 led to General Elphinstone's withdrawal from the Kabul garrison. One survivor reached Jellalabad on 13 January 1842. On 15 September 1842 the British army regained and destroyed parts of Kabul but then evacuated.

[l]   Cawnpore, place of the massacre by Nana Sahib at the strategic English garrison controlling the Grand Trunk Road between Delhi and the seat of government in Calcutta during the Indian Mutiny of 1857.

infamous; here is a test which will try our mettle, and show whether those who have pressed forward to share the government of the country have been prompted by a generous desire to assume functions which they could understand and discharge, or by an ignoble impatience of an inferiority of which their own failure will supply conclusive evidence. If India is governed as firmly and wisely as it has been conquered, we shall have done a great thing, and have taken a great step in marking the governing part of England with that imperial stamp which is essential to the dignity and self-respect of the rulers of half the world; but if we allow that great empire to be ruled in a petty spirit, and permit its greatest interests to be decided by the clamour of noisy speculators, or hot-headed and narrow-minded bigots, we shall have been guilty of a mean, illiberal action, and have shown a temper unworthy of the countrymen of those who, instead of turning empires into shops, raised factories into palaces.

The spirit of true liberalism has seldom been more nobly expressed than by one of the most illustrious of all liberals in reference to this very subject. 'Nothing under the sun', said M. de Tocqueville[m], 'was ever so extraordinary as the conquest, and above all as the government, of India by the English; nothing which from every part of the world more attracts men's attention to that little island the very name of which was unknown to the Greeks. Do you believe that after having filled such an immense space in the imagination of mankind, a people can retire from it with impunity? For my part I do not believe it. I think that the English obey a sentiment which is not only heroic, but just and truly conservative, in determining to keep India at any price, since they have got it. I add, that I am perfectly certain that they will keep it.'

India is but one instance of the problems which true liberals must solve successfully if their success is to be a blessing and not a curse. Hitherto they have been critics. They are now to be authors, and if they fail, their success will prove nothing but imbecility. There is hardly an institution in the country from

[m] Alexis de Tocqueville (1805–59), French political theorist and author of *Democracy in America* (1835 and 1840).

which good fruit is not to be got, if they will only catch the spirit which presided over its formation. In many cases, this has been done with great skill. Very many of the reforms which have succeeded each other so rapidly for the last thirty years have been liberal in the positive as well as the technical sense; but as the class which governs the country grows more numerous, and, as the slight and hasty opinions of persons who are doomed by their circumstances to a contented, and, for the most part, unconscious ignorance, gradually come to be invested with increasing importance, it becomes a matter of the first necessity to impress upon them the responsibilities under which they lie, and to give them, if possible, a glimpse of the sort of temper in which they must approach the great problems of government, if they are worthily to sustain the burden which eight centuries of greatness and glory have laid on their shoulders.

NATIONALITY
J. E. E. DALBERG-ACTON,
FIRST BARON ACTON*

Whatever great intellectual cultivation has been combined with that suffering which is inseparable from extensive changes in the condition of the people, men of speculative or imaginative genius have sought in the contemplation of an ideal society a remedy, or at least a consolation, for evils which they were practically unable to remove. Poetry has always preserved the idea, that at some distant time or place, in the Western islands or the Arcadian region, an innocent and contented people, free from the corruption and restraint of civilised life, have realised the legends of the golden age. The office of the poets is always nearly the same, and there is little variation in the features of their ideal world; but when philosophers attempt to admonish or reform mankind by devising an imaginary state, their motive is more definite and immediate, and their commonwealth is a satire as well as a model. Plato and Plotinus,[a] More[b] and Campanella,[c] constructed their fanciful societies with those materials which were omitted from the fabric of the actual communities, by the defects of which they were inspired. The Republic, the Utopia, and the City of the Sun, were protests against a state of things which the experience of their authors taught them to condemn, and from the faults of which they took refuge in the opposite extremes. They remained without

---

[*] J.E.E. Dalberg-Acton, *Home and Foreign Review* I, (1862), pp. 2–25.

[a] Plotinus (205–270 AD), Greek philosopher and chief exponent of Platonism during the third century AD.

[b] Sir Thomas More (1478–1535), Lord Chancellor and Humanist. His *Utopia* was first published in Latin in 1516.

[c] Tommaso Campanella (1568–1689), Italian philosopher and poet. His *The City of the Sun* was published in 1622.

influence, and have never passed from literary into political history, because something more than discontent and speculative ingenuity is needed, in order to invest a political idea with power over the masses of mankind. The scheme of a philosopher can command the practical allegiance of fanatics only, not of nations; and though oppression may give rise to violent and repeated outbreaks, like the convulsions of a man in pain, it cannot mature a settled purpose and plan of regeneration, unless a new notion of happiness is joined to the sense of present evil.

The history of religion furnishes a complete illustration. Between the later medieval sects and Protestantism there is an essential difference, that outweighs the points of analogy found in those systems which are regarded as heralds of the Reformation, and is enough to explain the vitality of the last in comparison with the others, Whilst Wycliffe[d] and Hus[e] contradicted certain particulars of the Catholic teaching, Luther rejected the authority of the Church, and gave to the individual conscience an independence which was sure to lead to an incessant resistance. There is a similar difference between the Revolt of the Netherlands, the Great Rebellion, the War of Independence, or the rising of Brabant,[f] on the one hand, and the French Revolution on the other. Before 1789, insurrections were provoked by particular wrongs, and were justified by definite complaints and by an appeal to principles which all men acknowledged. New theories were sometimes advanced in the cause of controversy, but they were accidental, and the great argument against tyranny was fidelity to the ancient laws. Since the change produced by the French Revolution, those aspirations which are awakened by the evils and defects of the

---

[d] John Wyclif (*c*.1329–84), challenged, *inter alia*, the teaching of the Catholic Church on the miracle of transubstantiation in the Mass, and also the Pope's position as head of the Church. Condemned for heresy in 1381.

[e] Jan Hus (1372/3–1415), Czech religious reformer. Taught Wyclif's doctrines in Bohemia. Condemned for heresy at the Council of Constance, 1414.

[f] Revolt of the Netherlands (1566–1648), against Spanish rule; The Great Rebellion (1642), marking the beginning of the English civil war; (American) War of Independence (1775–83); Brabant rising (1789–90), focus of the abortive Belgian revolt against the Austrian Hapsburgs.

social state have come to act as permanent and energetic forces throughout the civilised world. They are spontaneous and aggressive, needing no prophet to proclaim, no champion to defend them, but popular, unreasoning, and almost irresistible. The Revolution effected this change, partly by its doctrines, partly by the indirect influence of events. It taught the people to regard their wishes and wants as the supreme criterion of right. The rapid vicissitudes of power, in which each party successively appealed to the favour of the masses as the arbiter of success, accustomed the masses to be arbitrary as well as insubordinate. The fall of many governments, and the frequent redistribution of territory, deprived all settlements of the dignity of permanence. Tradition and prescription ceased to be guardians of authority; and the arrangements which proceeded from revolutions, from the triumphs of war, and from treaties of peace, were equally regardless of established rights. Duty cannot be dissociated from right, and nations refuse to be controlled by laws which are no protection.

In this condition of the world, theory and action follow close upon each other, and practical evils easily give birth to opposite systems. In the realms of free-will, the regularity of natural progress is preserved by the conflict of extremes. The impulse of the reaction carries men from one extremity towards another. The pursuit of a remote and ideal object, which captivates the imagination by its splendour and the reason by its simplicity, evokes an energy which would not be inspired by a rational, possible end, limited by many antagonistic claims, and confined to what is reasonable, practicable and just. One excess, or exaggeration, is the corrective of the other, and error promotes truth, where the masses are concerned, by counterbalancing a contrary error. The few have not strength to achieve great changes unaided; the many have not wisdom to be moved by truth unmixed. Where the disease is various, no particular definite remedy can meet the wants of all. Only the attraction of an abstract idea, or of an ideal state, can unite in a common action multitudes who seek a universal cure for many special evils, and a common restorative applicable to many different conditions. And hence false principles, which correspond with the bad as well as with the just aspirations of mankind, are a normal and necessary element in the social life of nations.

Theories of this kind are just, inasmuch as they are provoked by definite ascertained evils, and undertake their removal. They are useful in opposition, as a warning or a threat, to modify existing things, and keep awake the consciousness of wrong. They cannot serve as a basis for the reconstruction of civil society, as medicine cannot serve for food; but they may influence it with advantage, because they point out the direction, though not the measure, in which reform is needed. They oppose an order of things which is the result of a selfish and violent abuse of power by the ruling classes, and of artificial restriction on the natural progress of the world, destitute of an ideal element or a moral purpose. Practical extremes differ from the theoretical extremes they provoke, because the first are both arbitrary and violent, whilst the last, though also revolutionary, are at the same time remedial. In one case the wrong is voluntary, in the other it is inevitable. This is the general character of the contest between the existing order and the subversive theories that deny its legitimacy. There are three principal theories of this kind, impugning the present distribution of power, of property, and of territory, and attacking respectively the aristocracy, the middle class, and the sovereignty. They are the theories of equality, communism, and nationality. Though sprung from a common origin, opposing cognate evils, and connected by many links, they did not appear simultaneously. Rousseau [g] proclaimed the first Babœuf [h] the second, Mazzini [i] the third; and the third is the most recent in its appearance, the most attractive at the present time, and the richest in promise of future power.

In the old European system, the rights of nationalities were neither recognised by governments nor asserted by the people. The interests of the reigning families, not those of the nations, regulated the frontiers; and the administration was conducted

[g] Jean-Jacques Rousseau (1712-78), French political thinker, author of *The Social Contract* (1762).
[h] François Noël Baboeuf (1760-97), French revolutionary and egalitarian.
[i] Giuseppe Mazzini (1805-72), Italian revolutionary and patriot and founder of the Young Italy movement. Author of *The Duties of Man* (1860).

generally without any reference to popular desires. Where all liberties were suppressed, the claims of national independence were necessarily ignored, and a princess, in the words of Fénelon,[j] carried a monarchy in her wedding portion. The eighteenth century acquiesced in this oblivion of corporate rights on the Continent; for the absolutists cared only for the state, and the liberals only for the individual. The Church, the nobles, and the nation, had no place in the popular theories of the age; and they devised none in their own defence, for they were not openly attacked. The aristocracy retained its privileges, and the Church her property; and the dynastic interest, which overruled the natural inclination of the nations and destroyed their independence, nevertheless maintained their integrity. The national sentiment was not wounded in its most sensitive part. To dispossess a sovereign of his hereditary crown, and to annex his dominions, would have been held to inflict an injury upon all monarchies, and to furnish their subjects with a dangerous example, by depriving royalty of its inviolable character. In time of war, as there was no national cause at stake, there was no attempt to rouse national feeling. The courtesy of the rulers towards each other was proportionate to the contempt for the lower orders. Compliments passed between the commanders of hostile armies; there was no bitterness, and no excitement; battles were fought with the pomp and pride of a parade. The art of war became a slow and learned game. The monarchies were united not only by a natural community of interests, but by family alliances. A marriage contract sometimes became the signal for an interminable war, whilst family connections often set a barrier to ambition. After the wars of religion came to an end in 1648, the only wars were those which were waged for an inheritance or a dependency, or against countries whose system of government exempted them from the common law of dynastic states, and made them not only unprotected but obnoxious. These countries were England and Holland, until Holland ceased to be a republic, and until, in England, the defeat of the

---

[j] François de Salignac de La Mothe Fénelon (1651–1715), Roman Catholic theologian and Archbishop of Cambrai disgraced for his Quietist and mystical tendencies.

Jacobites in the Forty-five terminated the struggle for the crown. There was one country, however, which still continued to be an exception; one monarch whose place was not admitted in the comity of kings.

Poland did not possess those securities for stability which were supplied by dynastic connections, and the theory of legitimacy, wherever a crown could be obtained by marriage or inheritance. A monarch without royal blood, a crown bestowed by the nation, were an anomaly and an outrage in that age of dynastic absolutism. The country was excluded from the European system by the nature of its institutions. It excited a cupidity which could not be satisfied. It gave the reigning families of Europe no hope of permanently strengthening themselves by intermarriage with its rulers, or of obtaining it by bequest or by inheritance. The Hapsburgs had contested the possession of Spain and the Indies with the French Bourbons, of Italy with the Spanish Bourbons, of the empire with the house of Wittelsbach,[k] of Silesia with the house of Hohenzollern.[l] There had been wars between rival houses for half the territories of Italy and Germany. But none could hope to redeem their losses, or increase their power, in a country to which marriage and descent gave no claim. Where they could not permanently inherit, they endeavoured, by intrigues, to prevail at each election, and after contending in support of candidates who were their partisans, the neighbours at last appointed an instrument for the final demolition of the Polish state. Till then no nation had been deprived of its political existence by the Christian powers, and whatever disregard had been shown for national interests and sympathies, some care had been taken to conceal the wrong by a hypocritical perversion of law. But the partition of Poland was an act of wanton violence committed in open defiance not only of popular feeling but of public law. For the first time in modern history, a great state was suppressed, and a whole nation divided among its enemies.

---

[k] Wittelsbach, Bavarian dynasty which supported the empire during the Thirty Years War and was rewarded with the Palatinate in 1648.
[l] Hohenzollern, German dynasty which ruled in Brandenberg, Prussia, 1415–1918.

This famous measure, the most revolutionary act of the old absolutism, awakened the theory of nationality in Europe, converting a dormant right into an aspiration, and a sentiment into a political claim. 'No wise or honest man', wrote Edmund Burke, 'can approve of that partition, or can contemplate it without prognosticating great mischief from it to all countries at some future time.' Thenceforward there was a nation demanding to be united in a state, – a soul, as it were, wandering in search of a body in which to begin life over again; and, for the first time, a cry was heard that the arrangement of states was unjust – that their limits were unnatural, and that a whole people was deprived of its right to constitute an independent community. Before that claim could be efficiently asserted against the overwhelming power of its opponents, – before it gained energy, after the last partition, to overcome the influence of long habits of submission, and of the contempt which previous disorders had brought upon Poland, – the ancient European system was in ruins, and a new world was rising in its place. The old despotic policy which made the Poles its prey had two adversaries, – the spirit of English liberty, and the doctrines of that revolution which destroyed the French monarchy with its won weapons; and these two contradicted in contrary ways the theory that nations have no collective rights.

At the present day, the theory of nationality is not only the most powerful auxiliary of revolution, but its actual substance in the movements of the last three years. This, however, is a recent alliance, unknown to the first French Revolution. The modern theory of nationality arose partly as a legitimate consequence, partly as a reaction against it. As the system which overlooked national divisions was opposed by liberalism in two forms, the French and the English, so the system which insists upon them proceeds from two distinct sources, and exhibits the character either of 1688 or of 1789. When the French people abolished the authorities under which it lived, and became its own master, France was in danger of dissolution; for the common will is difficult to ascertain and does not readily agree. 'The laws', said Vergniaud,[m] in the debate on the sentence of the king, 'are obligatory only as the presumptive will of the people, which retains the right of approving or condemning them. The instant it manifests its wish, the work of the national representation, the law, must disappear.' This doctrine resolved society into its natural elements, and threatened to break up the country into as many republics as there were *communes*. For true republicanism is the principle of self-government in the whole and in all the parts. In an extensive country, it can prevail only by the union of several independent communities in a single confederacy, as in Greece, in Switzerland, in the Netherlands, and in America; so that a large republic not founded on the federal principle must result in the government of a single city, like Rome and Paris, and, in a less degree, Athens, Berne, and Amsterdam; or, in other words, a great democracy must either sacrifice self-government to unity, or preserve it by federalism.

The France of history fell together with the French state, which was the growth of centuries. The old sovereignty was destroyed. The local authorities were looked upon with aversion and alarm. The new central authority needed to be established on a new principle of unity. The state of nature, which was the ideal of society, was made the basis of the nation; descent was put in the place of tradition; and the French people was regarded as a physical product, – an ethnological, not historic, unit. It was assumed that a unity existed separate from the representation and the government, wholly independent of the past, and capable at any moment of expressing or of changing its mind. In the words of Sieyès,[n] it was no longer France, but some unknown country to which the nation was transported. The central power possessed authority, inasmuch as it obeyed the whole, and no divergence was permitted from the universal sentiment. This power, endowed with volition, was personified in the Republic One and Indivisible. The title signified that a part could not speak or act

[m]   Pierre Victurnier Vergniaud (1753–93), leader of the Girondists in the National Assembly of 1791.
[n]   Emmanuel Joseph Sieyès (1748–1836), French publicist and politician, advocate of nationalism at the time of the French Revolution.

for the whole, – that there was a power supreme over the state, distinct from, and independent of, its members; and it expressed, for the first time in history, the notion of an abstract nationality.

In this manner, the idea of the sovereignty of the people uncontrolled by the past gave birth to the idea of nationality independent of the political influence of history. It sprang from the rejection of the two authorities, – of the state and of the past. The kingdom of France was, geographically as well as politically, the product of a long series of events, and the same influences which built up the state formed the territory. The Revolution repudiated alike the agencies to which France owed her boundaries, and those to which she owed her government. Every effaceable trace and relic of national history was carefully wiped away, – the system of administration, the physical divisions of the country, the classes of society, the corporations, the weights and measures, the calendar. France was no longer bounded by the limits she had received from the condemned influence of her history; she could recognise only those which were set by nature. The definition of the nation was borrowed from the material world, and, in order to avoid a loss of territory, it became not only an abstraction, but a fiction.

There was a principle of nationality in the ethnological character of the movement, which is the source of the common observation that revolution is more frequent in Catholic than in Protestant countries. It is in fact more frequent in the Latin than in the Teutonic world, because it depends partly on a national impulse which is only awakened where there is an alien element, the vestige of a foreign domination, to expel. Western Europe has undergone two conquests, – one by the Romans, and one by the Germans, – and twice received laws from the invaders. Each time it rose again against the victorious race; and the two great reactions, while they differ according to the different characters of the two conquests, have the phenomenon of imperialism in common. The Roman republic laboured to crush the subjugated nations into a homogeneous and obedient mass; but the increase which the proconsular authority obtained in the process subverted the republican government, and the reaction of the provinces against Rome assisted in establishing the empire. The Cæsarean system gave an unprecedented freedom to the dependencies, and raised them to a civil equality which put an end to the dominion of race over race and of class over class. The monarchy was hailed as a refuge from the pride and cupidity of the Roman people; and the love of equality, the hatred of nobility, and the tolerance of despotism, implanted by Rome, became, at least in Gaul, the chief feature of the national character. But among the nations whose vitality had been broken down by the stern republic, not one retained the materials necessary to enjoy independence, or to develope [*sic.*] a new history. The political faculty which organises states and binds society in a moral order was exhausted, and the Christian doctors looked in vain over the waste of ruins for a people by whose aid the Church might survive the decay of Rome. A new element of national life was brought to that declining world by the enemies who destroyed it. The flood of barbarians settled over it for a season, and then subsided; and when the landmarks of civilisation appeared once more, it was found that the soil had been impregnated with a fertilising and regenerating influence, and that the inundation had laid the germs of future states and of a new society. The political sense and energy came with the new blood, and was exhibited in the power exercised by the younger race upon the old, and in the establishment of a graduated freedom. Instead of universal equal rights, the actual enjoyment of which is necessarily contingent on, and commensurate with, power, the rights of the people were made dependent on a variety of conditions, the first of which was the distribution of property. Civil society became a classified organism instead of a formless combination of atoms, and the feudal system gradually arose.

Roman Gaul had so thoroughly adopted the ideas of absolute authority and undistinguished equality during the five centuries between Cæsar and Clovis,° that the people could never be reconciled to the new system. Feudalism remained a foreign importation, and the feudal aristocracy an alien race, and the common people of France sought protection against both in the

---

°   Clovis, founder of the Kingdom of the Franks (*c*.466–511 AD).

Roman jurisprudence and the power of the crown. The development of absolute monarchy by the help of democracy is the one constant character of French history. The royal power, feudal at first, and limited by the immunities and the great vassals, became more popular as if grew more absolute; while the suppression of aristocracy, the removal of the intermediate authorities, was so particularly the object of the nation, that it was more energetically accomplished after the fall of the throne. The monarchy, which had been engaged from the thirteenth century in curbing the nobles, was at last thrust aside by the democracy, because it was too dilatory in the work, and was unable to deny its own origins and effectually ruin the class from which it sprung. All those things which constitute the peculiar character of the French Revolution, – the demand for equality, the hatred of nobility and feudalism, and of the Church which was connected within them, the constant reference to pagan examples, the suppression of monarchy, the new code of law, the breach with tradition, and the substitution of an ideal system for every thing that had proceeded from the mixture and mutual action of the races, – all these exhibit the common type of a reaction against the effects of the Frankish invasion. The hatred of royalty was less than the hatred of aristocracy; privileges were more detested than tyranny; and the king perished because of the origin of his authority, rather than because if its abuse. Monarchy unconnected with aristocracy became popular in France, even when most uncontrolled; whilst the attempt to reconstitute the throne, and to limit and fence it with its peers, broke down, because the old Teutonic elements on which it relied – hereditary nobility, primogeniture, and privilege – were no longer tolerated. The substance of the ideas of 1789 is not the limitation of the sovereign power, but the abrogation of intermediate powers. These powers, and the classes which enjoyed them, came in Latin Europe from a barbarian origin; and the movement which calls itself liberal is essentially national. If liberty were its object, its means would be the establishment of great independent authorities not derived from the state, and its model would be England. But its object is equality; and it seeks, like France in 1789, to cast out the elements of inequality which were introduced by the Teutonic race. This is the object which Italy and Spain have had in common with France, and herein consists the natural league of the Latin nations.

This national element in the movement was not understood by the revolutionary leaders. At first, their doctrine appeared entirely contrary to the idea of nationality. They taught that certain general principles of government were absolutely right in all states; and they asserted in theory the unrestricted freedom of the individual, and the supremacy of the will over every external necessity or obligation. This is in apparent contradiction to the national theory, that certain natural forces ought to determine the character, the form, and the policy of the state, by which a kind of fate is put in the place of freedom. Accordingly the national sentiment was not developed directly out of the revolution in which it was involved, but was exhibited first in resistance to it, when the attempt to emancipate had been absorbed in the desire to subjugate, and the republic had been succeeded by the empire. Napoleon called a new power into existence by attacking nationality in Russia, by delivering it in Italy, by governing in defiance of it in Germany and Spain. The sovereigns of these countries were deposed or degraded; and a system of administration was introduced, which was French in its origin, its spirit, and its instruments. The people resisted the change. The movement against it was popular and spontaneous, because the rulers were absent or helpless; and it was national, because it was directed against foreign institutions. In Tyrol, in Spain, and afterwards in Prussia, the people did not receive the impulse from the government, but undertook of their own accord to cast out the armies and the ideas of revolutionised France. Men were made conscious of the national element of the revolution by its conquests, not in its rise. The three things which the empire most openly oppressed – religion, national independence, and political liberty – united in a shortlived league to animate the great uprising by which Napoleon fell. Under the influence of that memorable alliance a political spirit was called forth on the Continent, which clung to freedom and abhorred revolution, and sought to restore, to develope [*sic.*], and to reform the decayed national institutions. The men who proclaimed these ideas, Stein [p] and Görres,[q] Humboldt,[r] Müller,[s] and De Maistre,[2t] were as hostile to Bonapartism as to the absolutism of the old governments, and insisted on the national rights, which had been invaded equally by both, and which they hoped to restore by the destruction of the French supremacy.

With the cause that triumphed at Waterloo the friends of the revolution had no sympathy, for they had learned to identify their doctrine with the cause of France. The Holland-House

[2] There are some remarkable thoughts on nationality in the state papers of the Count de Maistre. 'En premier lieu les nations sont quelque chose dans le monde, il n'est pas permis de les compter pour rien, de les affliger dans leurs convenances dans leurs affections, dans leurs intérêts les plus chers...On le traités du 30 mai anéantit complétement la Savoire; il divise l'indivisible; il partage en trois portions une malheureuse nation de 4000,000 hommes, une par la langue, une par la religion, une par le caractère, une par l'habitude invétérée, une entin par les limites naturelles...L'union des nations ne souffre pas de difficultés sur la carte géographique; mais dans la réalité, c'est autre chose; il y a des nations *immiseibles*...je lui parlai par occasion de l'esprit italien qui s'agite dans ce moment; il (Count Nesselrode) me répondit : 'Oui, monsieur; mais cet esprit est un grand mal, car il peut géner les arrangements de l'Italie'' (*Correspondance Diplomatique de J. de Maistre*, ii. 7, 8, 21, 25). In the same year, 1815, Görres wrote: 'In Italien wie allerwärts ist das Volk geweekt; es will etwas grossartiges, es will Ideen haben, die, wenn es sie auch nicht ganz begreift dech einen frein nnend-lichen Gesichtskreis seiner Einbildung eröffnen...Es ist reiner Naturtrieb das ein Volk, also scharf und deutlich in seine natürlichen Gränzen eingeschlossen, aus der Zerstreuung in die Einheit sich zu sammeln sucht' (*Wirke*, ii. 20).

[p] Friedrich Karl Freiherr (Baron) von Stein (1757–1831), Prussian Liberal statesman and nationalist who, as Chief Minister, played a major role in the rehabilitation of Prussia after the French defeat in 1806.

[q] Johann Joseph von Görres (1776–1848), German writer and focus of the national movement. Critic of absolutism and Professor of Literature at Munich from 1827.

[r] Wilhelm von Humboldt (1767–1835), Prussian liberal thinker and educational reformer, author of *Some Ideas Concerning the Attempt to Define the Limits of State Action* (1792).

[s] Adam Müller (1779–1829), Romantic political thinker, born in Prussia, author of *Elements of Politics* (1809).

[t] Joseph de Maistre (1753–1821), Savoyard critic of the Enlightenment and French Revolution. Author of *Considerations on France* (1796); also *The Pope, St Petersburg Dialogues*, both written in Russia between 1892 and 1817.

Whigs in England,[u] the Afrancesados[v] in Spain, the Muratists in Italy,[w] and the partisans of the Confederation of the Rhine,[x] merging patriotism in their revolutionary affections, regretted the fall of the French power, and looked with alarm at those new and unknown forces which the War of Deliverance had evoked, and which were as menacing to French liberalism as to French supremacy. But the new aspirations for national and popular rights were crushed at the restoration. The liberals of those days cared for freedom, not in the shape of national independence, but of French institutions; and they combined against the nations with the ambition of the governments. They were as ready to sacrifice nationality to their ideal, as the Holy Alliance[y] was to the interests of absolutism. Talleyrand[z] indeed declared at Vienna that the Polish question ought to have precedence over all other questions, because the partition of Poland had been one of the first and greatest causes of the evils which Europe had suffered; but dynastic interests prevailed. All the sovereigns represented at Vienna recovered their dominions, except the King of Saxony,[aa] who was punished for his fidelity to Napoleon; but the states that were unrepresented in the reigning families – Poland, Venice, and Genoa – were

[u] Holland House Whigs, Whig politicians and men of letters led by Henry Richard Vassal Fox (1773–1840). Propagated the liberal ideas of Foxite Whigs who were moderately sympathetic to the French revolutionaries.

[v] Afrancesados, Spanish supporters of France during the Spanish War of Independence (1808–14).

[w] Muratists, Neopolitan followers of Joachim Murat (1767–1815). Born in France, son of an innkeeper, he was made king of Naples by Napoleon in 1808. However, he abandoned the emperor in 1813 and lost his throne in 1814.

[x] Confederation Of The Rhine. Founded on 12 July 1806 on the initiative of Napoleon, it composed sixteen south and west German states. Its aim was the domination of west Germany by France on the dissolution of the Holy Roman Empire.

[y] Holy Alliance. A pact made on 26 September 1815 between Russia, Austria, and Prussia. The rulers of these states undertook to be guided solely by Christian principles. Designed to halt the spread of political liberty following the French Revolution.

[z] Perigord Charles Maurice de Talleyrand (1754–1838), French statesman in the First Estate and then the National Assembly. Influential in the passing of the decree which nationalized church properties. Foreign Minister (1797–1807) and again under Louis XVIII.

[aa] Frederick Augustus I (1763–1827).

not revived, and even the Pope had great difficulty in recovering the Legations from the grasp of Austria. Nationality, which the old *régime* had ignored, which had been outraged by the revolution and the empire, received, after its first open demonstration, the hardest blow at the Congress of Vienna. The principle which the first partition had generated, to which the revolution had given a basis of theory, which had been lashed by the empire into a momentary convulsive effort, was matured by the long error of the restoration into a consistent doctrine, nourished and justified by the situation of Europe.

The governments of the Holy Alliance devoted themselves to suppress with equal care the revolutionary spirit by which they had been threatened, and the national spirit by which they had been restored. Austria, which owed nothing to the national movement, and had prevented its revival after 1809, naturally took the lead in repressing it. Every disturbance of the final settlements of 1815, every aspiration for changes or reforms, was condemned as sedition. This system repressed the good with the evil tendencies of the age; and the resistance which it provoked during the generation that passed away from the restoration to the fall of Metternich,[bb] and again under the reaction which commenced with Schwarzenberg[cc] and ended with the administrations of Bach [dd] and Manteuffel,[ee] proceeded from various combinations of the opposite forms of liberalism. In the successive phases of that struggle, the idea that national

[bb] Prince Klemens Wenzel Lothar von Metternich (1773–1859), Austrian statesman and Minister of Foreign Affairs, 1809. At the Congress of Vienna he convinced the European powers that Austria was essential for the European balance of power. Supporter of autocracy and police despotism at home and abroad.

[cc] Prince Felix Ludwig Johann Friedrich Schwarzenberg (1800–52), Austrian diplomat, politician, and minister. Advocate of Hapsburg leadership in central Europe. As Prime Minister in 1848 he called in the Russians to repress the Hungarians. Introduced centralized absolutism in 1851.

[dd] Alexander von Bach (1813–93). Austrian minister of the interior and one of the few liberals willing to serve under Schwarzenberg. Responsible for the 'Bach system' of extreme centralization and bureaucratic control of the Hapsburg empire.

[ee] Edwin von Manteuffel (1809–85). Prussian field-marshal and (very unpopular) first German governor of Alsace-Lorraine.

claims are above all other rights gradually rose to the supremacy which it now possesses among the revolutionary agencies.

The first liberal movement, that of the Carbonari [ff] in the South of Europe, had no specific national character, but was supported by the Bonapartists both in Spain and Italy. In the following years, the opposite ideas of 1813 came to the front, and a revolutionary movement, in many respects hostile to the principles of revolution, began in defence of liberty, religion, and nationality. All these cases were united in the Irish agitation, and in the Greek, Belgian, and Polish revolutions. Those sentiments which had been insulted by Napoleon, and had risen against him, rose against the governments of the restoration. They had been oppressed by the sword, and then by the treaties. The national principle added force, but not justice, to this movement, which, in every case, but Poland, was successful. A period followed in which it degenerated into a purely national idea, as the agitation for repeal succeeded emancipation, and Panslavism and Panhellenism arose under the auspices of the Eastern Church. This was the third phase of the resistance to the settlement of Vienna, which was weak, because it failed to satisfy national or constitutional aspirations, either of which would have been a safeguard against the other, by a moral if not by a popular justification. At first, in 1813, the people rose against their conquerors, in defence of their legitimate rulers. They refused to be governed by usurpers. In the period 1825 and 1831, they resolved that they would not be misgoverned by strangers. The French administration was often better than that which it displaced; but there were prior claimants for the authority exercised by the French, and at first the national contest was a contest for legitimacy. In the second period this element was wanting. No dispossessed princes led the Greeks, the Belgians, or the Poles. The Turks, the Dutch, and the Russians were attacked, not as usurpers, but as oppressors, – because they misgoverned, not because they were of a different race. Then began a time when the text simply

---

[ff] Carbonarism, a movement, composed of secret societies which developed in southern Italy and became the main focus of opposition after the Bourbon restoration (1815), albeit with no clear aims.

was, that nations would not be governed by foreigners. Power legitimately obtained, and exercised with moderation, was declared invalid. National rights, like religion, had borne part in the previous combinations, and had been auxiliaries in the struggles for freedom, but now nationality became a paramount claim, which was to assert itself alone, which might put forward as pretexts the rights of rulers, the liberties of the people, the safety of religion, but which, if no such union could be formed, was to prevail at the expense of every other cause for which nations make sacrifices.

Metternich is, next to Napoleon, the chief promoter of this theory; for the anti-national character of the restoration was most distinct in Austria, and it is in opposition to the Austrian government that nationality grew into a system. Napoleon, who, trusting to his armies, despised moral forces in politics, was overthrown by their rising. Austria committed the same fault in the government of her Italian provinces. The kingdom of Italy had united all the northern part of the Peninsula in a single state; and the national feelings, which the French repressed elsewhere, were encouraged as a safeguard of their power in Italy and in Poland. When the tide of victory turned, Austria invoked against the French the aid of the new sentiment they had fostered. Nugent[gg] announced, in his proclamation to the Italians, that they should become an independent nation. The same spirit served different masters, and contributed first to the destruction of the old states, then to the expulsion of the French, and again, under Charles Albert, to a new revolution. It was appealed to in the name of the most contradictory principles of government, and served all parties in succession, because it was one in which all could unite. Beginning by a protest against the dominion of race over race, its mildest and least-developed form, it grew into a condemnation of every state that included different races, and finally became the complete and consistent theory, that the state and the nation must be coextensive. 'It is', says Mr. Mill, 'in general a necessary condition of free institutions, that the boundaries of

---

[gg]   Count Lavall Nugent (1777–1862). Prince of the Holy Roman Empire and Austrian field–marshall of Irish descent.

governments should coincide in the main with those of nationalities.'[3]

The outward historical progress of this idea from an indefinite aspiration to be the keystone of a political system, may be traced in the life of the man who gave to it the element in which its strength resides, – Giuseppe Mazzini. He found Carbonarism impotent against the measures of the governments, and resolved to give new life to the liberal movement by transferring it to the ground of nationality. Exile is the nursery of nationality, as oppression is the school of liberalism; and Mazzini conceived the idea of Young Italy[hh] when he was a refugee at Marseilles. In the same way, the Polish exiles are the champions of every national movement; for to them all political rights are absorbed in the idea of independence, which, however, they may differ with each other, is the one aspiration common to them all. Towards the year 1830, literature also contributed to the national idea. 'It was the time', says Mazzini, 'of the great conflict between the romantic and the classical school, which might with equal truth be called a conflict between the partisans of freedom and authority.' The romantic school was infidel in Italy, and Catholic in Germany; but in both it had the common effect of encouraging national history and literature, and Dante was as great an authority with the Italian democrats as with the leaders of the medieval revival at Vienna, Munich, and Berlin. But neither the influence of the exiles, nor that of the poets and critics of the new party, extended over the masses. It was a sect without popular sympathy or encouragement, a conspiracy founded not on a grievance, but on a doctrine; and when the attempt to rise was made in Savoy, in 1834, under a banner with the motto 'Unity, Independence, God and Humanity', the people were puzzled at its object, and indifferent to its failure. But Mazzini continued his propaganda, developed his Giovine

---

[3]   *Considerations on Representative Government*, p. 298.
[hh]   Young Italy (Giovane Italia), a new Liberal league founded by Mazzini in 1832 for the unification of Italy.

Italia into a Giovine Europa,[ii] and established in 1847 the international league of nations. 'The people', he said, in his opening address, 'is penetrated with only one idea, that of unity and nationality...There is no international question as to forms of government, but only a national question.'

The revolution of 1848, unsuccessful in its national purpose, prepared the subsequent victories of nationality in two ways. The first of these was the restoration of the Austrian power in Italy, with a new and more energetic centralisation, which give no promise of freedom. Whilst that system prevailed, the right was on the side of the national aspirations, and they were revived in a more complete and cultivated form by Manin.[ij] The policy of the Austrian government, which failed during the ten years of the reaction to convert the tenure by force into a tenure by right, and to establish with free institutions the condition of allegiance, gave a negative encouragement to the theory. It deprived Francis Joseph of all active support and sympathy in 1859; for he was more clearly wrong in his conduct than his enemies in their doctrines. The real cause of the energy which the national theory has acquired is, however, the triumph of the democratic principle in France, and its recognition by the European powers. The theory of nationality is involved in the democratic theory of the sovereignty of the general will. 'One hardly knows what any division of the human race should be free to do, if not to determine with which of the various collective bodies of human beings they choose to associate themselves.'[4] It is by this act that a nation constitutes itself. To have a collective will, unity is necessary; and independence is requisite in order to assert it. Unity and nationality are still more essential to the notion of the sovereignty of the people than the cashiering of monarchs, or the revocation of laws. Arbitrary acts of this kind may be

ii   Young Europe (Giovane Europa), an alliance on Mazzinian lines for information and propaganda purposes formed in Switzerland by republicans from Italy, Germany, and Poland in 1834.

ij   Daniel Manin (1804–57), Italian lawyer and patriot who inspired the defence of Venice against the Austrian army in 1848. Influential thereafter in the formation of the Italian National Society.

4   Mill's Considerations, p. 296.

prevented by the happiness of the people, or the popularity of the king; but a nation inspired by the democratic idea cannot with consistency allow a part of itself to belong to a foreign state, or the whole to be divided into several native states. The theory of nationality therefore proceeds from both the principles which divided the political world from legitimacy, which ignores its claims, and from the revolution, which assumes them; and for the same reason it is the chief weapon of the last against the first.

In pursuing the outward and visible growth of the national theory, we are prepared for an examination of its political character and value. The absolutism which has created it denies equally that absolute right of national unity which is a product of democracy, and that claim of national liberty which belongs to the theory of freedom. These two views of nationality, corresponding to the French and to the English systems, are connected in name only, and are in reality the opposite extremes of political thought. In one case, nationality is founded on the perpetual supremacy of the collective will, of which the unity of the nation is the necessary condition, to which every other influence must defer, and against which no obligation enjoys authority, and all resistance is tyrannical. The nation is here an ideal unit founded on the race, in defiance of the modifying action of external causes, of tradition, and of existing rights. It overrules the rights and wishes of the inhabitants, absorbing their divergent interests in a fictitious unity; sacrifices their several inclinations and duties to the higher claim of nationality; and crushes all natural rights and all established liberties, for the purpose of vindicating itself.[5] Whenever a single definite object is made the supreme end of the state, be it the advantage of a class, the safety or the power of the country, the greatest happiness of the greatest number, or the support of any speculative idea, the state becomes for the

---

[5] 'Le sentiment d'indépendance nationale est encore plus général et plus profondément gravé dans le cœur des peuples que l'amour d'une liberté constitutionnelle. Les nations les plus soumises au despotisme éprouvent ce sentiment avec autant de vivacité que les nations libres; les peuples les plus barbares le sentent même encore plus vivement que les nations policées.' *L'Italie au Dix-neuvième Siècle*, p. 148, Paris, 1821.

time inevitably absolute. Liberty alone demands for its realisation the limitation of the public authority; for liberty is the only object which benefits all authority; for liberty is the only object which benefits all alike, and provokes no sincere opposition. In supporting the claims of national unity, governments must be subverted in whose title there is no flaw, and whose policy is beneficent and equitable, and subjects must be compelled to transfer their allegiance to an authority for which they have no attachment, and which may be practically a foreign domination.

Connected with this theory in nothing except in the common enmity of the absolute state, is the theory which represents nationality as an essential, but not a supreme, element in determining the forms of the state. It is distinguished from the other, because it tends to diversity and not to uniformity, to harmony and not to unity; because it aims not at an arbitrary change, but at careful respect for the existing conditions of political life; and because it obeys the laws and results of history, not the aspirations of an ideal future. While the theory of unity makes the nation a source of despotism and revolution, the theory of liberty regards it as the bulwark of self-government, and the foremost limit to the excessive power of the state. Private rights, which are sacrificed to the unity, are preserved by the union, of nations. No power can so efficiently resist the tendencies of centralisation, of corruption, and of absolutism, as that community which is the vastest that can be included in a state, which imposes on its members a consistent similarity of character, interest, and opinion, and which arrests the action of the sovereign by the influence of a divided patriotism. The presence of different nations under the same sovereignty is similar in its effect to the independence of the Church in the state. It provides against the servility which flourishes under the shadow of a single authority, by balancing interests, multiplying associations, and giving to the subject the restraint and support of a combined opinion. In the same way it promotes independence, by forming definite groups of public opinion, and by affording a great source and centre of political sentiments, and of notions of duty not derived from the sovereign will. Liberty provokes diversity, and diversity preserves liberty by supplying the means of organisation. All those portions of law which govern the relations of men with each other, and regulate social life, are the varying result of national custom, and the creation of private society. In these things, therefore, the several nations will differ from each other; for they themselves have produced them, and they do not owe them to the state which rules them all. This diversity in the same state is a firm barrier against the intrusion of the government beyond the political sphere which is common to all, into the social department which escapes legislation and is ruled by spontaneous laws. This sort of interference is characteristic of an absolute government, and is sure to provoke a reaction, and finally a remedy. That intolerance of social freedom which is natural to absolutism, is sure to find a corrective in the national diversities, which no other force could so efficiently provide. The coexistence of several nations under the same state is a test, as well as the best security, of its freedom. It is also one of the chief instruments of civilisation; and, as such, it is in the natural and providential order, and indicates a state of greater advancement than the national unity which is the ideal of modern liberalism.

The combination of different nations in one state is as necessary a condition of civilised life as the combination of men in society. Inferior races are raised by living in political union with races intellectually superior. Exhausted and decaying nations are revived by the contact of a younger vitality. Nations in which the elements of organisation and the capacity for government have been lost, either through the demoralising influence of despotism, or the disintegrating action of democracy, are restored and educated anew under the discipline of a stronger and less corrupted race. This fertilising and regenerating process can only be obtained by living under one government. It is in the cauldron of the state that the fusion takes place by which the vigour, the knowledge, and the capacity of one portion of mankind may be communicated to another. Where political and national boundaries coincide, society ceases to advance, and nations relapse into a condition corresponding to that of men who renounce intercourse with their fellow-men. The difference between the two unites mankind not only by the benefits it confers in those who live together, but because it connects society either by a political or a national bond, gives to every people an interest in its neighbours, either because they are under the same government or because they are of the same race, and thus promotes the interests of humanity, of civilisation, and of religion.

Christianity rejoices at the mixture of races, as paganism identifies itself with their differences, because truth is universal, and errors various and particular. In the ancient world idolatry and nationality went together, and the same term is applied in Scripture to both. It was the mission of the Church to overcome national differences. The period of her undisputed supremacy was that in which all Western Europe obeyed the same laws, all literature was contained in one language, and the political unity of Christendom was personified in a single potentate, while its intellectual unity was represented in one university.[kk] As the ancient Romans concluded their conquests by carrying away the gods of the conquered people, Charlemagne overcame the national resistance of the Saxons only by the forcible destruction of their pagan rites.[ll] Out of the medieval period, and the combined action of the German race and the Church,[mm] came forth a new system of nations, and a new conception of nationality. Nature was overcome in the nation as well as in the individual. In pagan and uncultivated times, nations were distinguished from each other by the widest diversity, not only in religion, but in customs, language, and character. Under the new law they had many things in common; the old barriers which separated them were removed, and the new principle of self-government, which Christianity imposed, enabled them to live together under the same authority, without necessarily losing their cherished habits, their customs, or their laws. The new idea of freedom made room for different races in one state. A nation was no longer what it had been to the ancient world, – the progeny of a common ancestor, or the aboriginal product of a particular region, – a result of merely physical and material causes, – but

[kk] University of Paris.
[ll] Charlemagne (742–814), Emperor of the Franks. Conquered and converted the Saxons, thus removing a persistent threat to the Papacy and a united Christian Europe.
[mm] Holy Roman Empire (1254–1806).

a moral and political being; not the creation of geographical or physiological unity, but developed in the course of history by the action of the state. It is derived from the state, not supreme over it. A state may in course of time produce a nationality; but that a nationality should constitute a state is contrary to the nature of modern civilisation. The nation derives its rights and its power from the memory of a former independence.

The Church has agreed in this respect with the tendency of political progress, and discouraged wherever she could the isolation of nations; admonishing them of their duties to each other, and regarding conquest and feudal investiture as the natural means of raising barbarous or sunken nations to a higher level. But though she has never attributed to national independence an immunity from the accidental consequences of feudal law, of hereditary claims, or of testamentary arrangements, she defends national liberty against uniformity and centralisation, with an energy inspired by perfect community of interests. For the same enemy threatens both; and the state which is reluctant to tolerate differences, and to do justice to the peculiar character of various races, must from the same cause interfere in the internal government of religion. The connection of religious liberty with the emancipation of Poland or Ireland is not merely the accidental result of local causes; and the failure of the Concordat to unite the subjects of Austria is the natural consequence of a policy which did not desire to protect the provinces in their diversity and autonomy, and sought to bribe the Church by favours, instead of strengthening her by independence. From this influence of religion in modern history has proceeded a new definition of patriotism.

The difference between nationality and the state is exhibited in the nature of patriotic attachment. Our connection with the race is merely natural or physical, whilst our duties to the political nation are ethical. One is a community of affections and instincts infinitely important and powerful in savage life, but pertaining more to the animal than to the civilised man; the other is an authority governing by laws, imposing obligations, and giving a moral sanction and character to the natural relations of society. Patriotism is in political life what faith is in religion, and it stands to the domestic feelings and to homesickness as faith to fanaticism and to superstition. It has one aspect derived from private life and nature; for it is an extension of the family affections, as the tribe is an extension of the family. But in its real political character, patriotism consists in the development of the instinct of self-preservation into a moral duty which may involve self-sacrifice. Self-preservation is both an instinct and a duty, natural and involuntary in one respect, and at the same time a moral obligation. By the first it produces the family; by the last, the state. If the nation could exist without the state, subject only to the instinct of self-preservation, it would be incapable of denying, controlling, or sacrificing itself; it would be an end and a rule to itself. But in the political order moral purposes are realised, and public ends are pursued, to which private interests and even existence must be sacrificed. The great sign of true patriotism, the development of selfishness into sacrifice, is the product of political life. That sense of duty which is supplied by race is not entirely separated from its selfish and instinctive basis; and the love of country, like married love, stands at the same time on a material and a moral foundation. The patriot must distinguish between the two causes or objects of his devotion. The attachment which is given only to the country is like obedience given only to the state – a submission to physical influences. The man who prefers his country before every other duty shows the same spirit as the man who surrenders every right to the state. They both deny that right is superior to authority. There is a moral and political country, in the language of Burke, distinct from the geographical, which may be possibly in collision with it. The Frenchmen who bore arms against the Convention were as patriotic as the Englishmen who bore arms against King Charles; for they recognised a higher duty than that of obedience to the actual sovereign. 'In an address to France', said Burke, 'in an attempt to treat with it, or in considering any scheme at all relative to it, it is impossible we should mean the geographical, we must always mean the moral and political, country...The truth is, that France is out of itself – the moral France is separated from the geographical. The master of the house is expelled, and the robbers are in possession. If we look for the corporate people of France, existing as corporate in the eye and intention of

public law (that corporate people, I mean, who are free to
deliberate and to decide, and who have a capacity to treat and
conclude) they are in Flanders, and Germany, in Switzerland,
Spain, Italy, and England.[nn] There are all the princes of the
blood, there are all the orders of the state, there are all the
parliaments of the kingdom...I am sure that if half that number
of the same description were taken out of this country, it would
leave hardly any thing that I should call the people of
England.'[6] Rousseau draws nearly the same distinction between
the country to which we happen to belong, and that which
fulfils towards us the political functions of the state. In the
Emile [oo] he has a sentence, of which it is not easy in a
translation to convey the point: 'Qui n'a pas une patrie a du
moins au pays.' And in his tract on Political economy he
writes: 'How shall men love their country, if it is nothing more
for them than for strangers, and bestows on them only that
which it can refuse to none?' It is in the same sense he says
further on, 'La patrie ne peut subsister sans la liberté.'[7]

6   Burke's Remarks on the Policy of the Allies [with Respect to France,
    1793, *Works*, VII, pp. 139–41], *Works*, v. 26, 29, 30.
nn In the two months following the fall of the Bastille, 'some 20,000 passports
    were delivered' as the privileged classes fled across the frontier. A.
    Cobban, *A History of Modern France*, I, *1715–1799* (1957;
    Harmondsworth: Penguin, 1963), p. 151.
oo The sentence is best clarified within a larger quotation: [Tutor] 'Liberty is
    not to be found in any form of government, she is in the heart of the free
    man, he bears her with him everywhere...
    'If I spoke to you of the duties of a citizen, you would perhaps ask me,
    "Which is my country?" And you would think you had put me to
    confusion. Yet you would be mistaken, dear Emile, for he who has no
    country has, at least, the land in which he lives. There is always a
    government and certain so-called laws under which he has lived in
    peace...' J. J. Rousseau, *Emile* (1762), transl. B. Foxley (London: Dent,
    1911), p. 437.
7   Œuvres, ii. 717, I. 593, 595. Bousset, in a passage of great beauty, on the
    love of country, does not attain to the political definition of the word. "La
    société humaine demande qu'on aime la terre ou l'on habite ensemble, on
    la regarde comme une mère et une nourrice commune...Les hommes en
    effet se sentent liés par quelque chose de fort, lorsque'ils songent, que la
    même terre qui les a portés et nourris étant vivants, les recevra dans son
    sein quand ils seront morts." *Politique tiree de l'Ecriture Sainte*, –
    Œuvres, x. 317.

The nationality formed by the state, then, is the only one to which we owe political duties, and it is therefore the only one which has political rights. The Swiss are ethnologically either French, Italian, or German; but no nationality has the slightest claim upon them, except the purely political nationality of Switzerland. The Tuscan or the Neapolitan state has formed a nationality; but the citizens of Florence and of Naples have no political community with each other. There are other states which have neither succeeded in absorbing distinct races in a political nationality, nor in separating a particular district from a larger nation. Austria and Mexico are instances on the one hand, Parma and Baden on the other. The progress of civilisation deals hardly with the last description of states. In order to maintain their integrity, they must attach themselves by confederations, or family alliances, to greater powers, and thus lose something of their independence. Their tendency is to isolate and shut off their inhabitants, to narrow the horizon of their views, and to dwarf in some degree the proportions of their ideas. Public opinion cannot maintain its liberty and purity in such small dimensions, and the currents that come from larger communities sweep over a contracted territory. In a small and homogeneous population there is hardly room for a natural classification of society, or for inner groups of interests that set bounds to sovereign power. The government and the subjects contend with borrowed weapons. The resources of the one, and the aspirations of the other, are derived from some external source; and the consequence is that the country becomes the instrument and the scene of contests in which it is not interested. These states, like the minuter communities of the Middle Ages, serve a purpose, by constituting partitions and securities of self-government in the larger states; but they are impediments to the progress of society, which depends on the mixture of races under the same governments.

The vanity and peril of national claims founded on no political tradition, but on race alone, appear in Mexico. There the races are divided by blood, without being grouped together in different regions. It is therefore neither possible to unite them, nor to convert them into the elements of an organised state. They are fluid, shapeless, and unconnected, and cannot be precipitated, or formed into the basis of political institutions.

As they cannot be used by the state, they cannot be recognised by it; and their peculiar qualities, capabilities, passions, and attachments, are of no service, and therefore obtain no regard. They are necessarily ignored, and are therefore perpetually outraged. From this difficulty of races with political pretensions but without political position, the Eastern world escaped by the institution of castes. Where there are only two races, there is the resource of slavery; but when different races inhabit the different territories of an empire composed of several smaller states, it is of all possible combinations the most favourable to the establishment of a highly-developed system of freedom. In Austria there are two circumstances which add to the difficulty of the problem, but also increase its importance. The several nationalities are at very unequal degrees of advancement, and there is no single nation which is so predominant as to overwhelm or absorb the others. These are the conditions necessary for the very highest degree of organisation which government is capable of receiving. They supply the greatest variety of intellectual resource; the perpetual incentive to progress, which is afforded not merely by competition, but by the spectacle of a more advanced people; the most abundant elements of self-government, combined with the impossibility for the state to rule all by its own will, and the fullest security for the preservation of local customs and ancient rights. In such a country as this, liberty would achieve its most glorious results, while centralisation and absolutism would be destruction.

The problem presented to the government of Austria is higher than that which is solved in England, because of the necessity of admitting the national claims. The parliamentary system fails to provide for them, as it presupposes the unity of the people. Hence in those countries in which different races dwell together, it has not satisfied their desires, and is regarded as an imperfect form of freedom. It brings out more clearly than before the differences it does not recognise, and thus continues the work of the old absolutism, and appears as a new phase of centralisation. In those countries, therefore, the power of the imperial parliament must be limited as jealously as the power of the crown, and many of its functions must be discharged by provincial diets, and a descending series of local authorities.

The great importance of nationality in the state consists in the fact that is the basis of political capacity. The character of a nation determines in great measure the form and vitality of the state. Certain political habits and ideas belong to particular nations, and they vary with the course of the national history. A people just emerging from barbarism, a people effete from the excesses of a luxurious civilisation, cannot possess the means of governing itself; a people devoted to equality, or to absolute monarchy, is incapable of producing an aristocracy; a people averse to the institution of private property is without the first element of freedom. Each of these can be converted into efficient members of a free community only by the contact of a superior race, in whose power will lie the future prospects of the state. A system which ignores these things, and does not rely for its support on the character and aptitude of the people, does not intend that they should administer their own affairs, but that they should simply be obedient to the supreme command. The denial of nationality, therefore, implies the denial of political liberty.

The greatest adversary of the rights of nationality is the modern theory of nationality. By making the state and the nation commensurate with each other in theory, it reduces practically to a subject condition all other nationalities that may be within the boundary. It cannot admit them to an equality with the ruling nation which constitutes the state, because the state would then cease to be national, which would be a contradiction of the principle of its existence. According, therefore, to the degree of humanity and civilisation in that dominant body which claims all the rights of the community, the inferior races are exterminated, or reduced to servitude, or outlawed, or put in a condition of dependence.

If we take the establishment of liberty for the realisation of moral duties to be the end of civil society, we must conclude that those states are substantially the most perfect which, like the British and Austrian empires, include various distinct nationalities without oppressing them. Those in which no mixture of races has occurred are imperfect; and those in which its effects have disappeared are decrepit. A state which is incompetent to satisfy different races condemns itself; a state which labours to neutralise, to absorb, or to expel them, destroys its own vitality; a state which does not include them is destitute of the chief basis of self-government. The theory of nationality, therefore, is a retrograde step in history. It is the most advanced form of the revolution, and must retain its power to the end of the revolutionary period, of which it announces the approach. Its great historical importance depends on two chief causes.

First, it is a chimera. The settlement at which it aims is impossible. As it can never be satisfied and exhausted, and always continues to assert itself, it prevents the government from ever relapsing into the condition which provoked its rise. The danger is too threatening, and the power over men's minds too great, to allow any system to endure which justifies the resistance of nationality. It must contribute, therefore, to obtain that which in theory it condemns, – the liberty of different nationalities as members of one sovereign community. This is a service which no other force could accomplish; for it is a corrective alike of absolute monarchy, of democracy, and of constitutionalism, as well as of the centralisation which is common to all three. Neither the monarchical, nor the revolutionary, nor the parliamentary system can do this; and all the ideas which have excited enthusiasm in past times are impotent for the purpose, except nationality alone.

And secondly, the national theory marks the end of the revolutionary doctrine, and its logical exhaustion. In proclaiming the supremacy of the rights of nationality, the system of democratic equality goes beyond its own extreme boundary, and falls into contradiction with itself. Between the democratic and the national phase of the revolution, socialism had intervened, and had already carried the consequences of the principle to an absurdity. But that phase was passed. The revolution survived its offspring, and produced another further result. Nationality is more advanced than socialism, because it is a more arbitrary system. The social theory endeavours to provide for the existence of the individual, beneath the terrible burdens which modern society heaps upon labour. It is not merely a development of the notion of equality, but a refuge from real misery and starvation. However false the solution, it was a reasonable demand that the poor should be saved from destruction; and if the freedom of the state was sacrificed to the safety of the individual, the more immediate object was, at least in theory, attained. But nationality does not aim either at liberty or prosperity, both of which it sacrifices to the imperative necessity of making the nation the mould and measure of the state. Its course will be marked with material as well as moral ruin, in order that a new invention may prevail over the works of God and the interests of mankind. There is no principle of change, no phase of political speculation conceivable, more comprehensive, more subversive, or more arbitrary than this. It is a confutation of democracy, because it sets limits to the exercise of the popular will, and substitutes for it a higher principle. It prevents not only the division, but the extension of the state, and forbids to terminate war by conquest, and to obtain a security for peace. Thus, after surrendering the individual to the collective will, the revolutionary system makes the collective will subject to conditions which are independent of it; and rejects all law, only to be controlled by an accident.

Although, therefore, the theory of nationality is more absurd and more criminal than the theory of socialism, it has an important mission in the world, and marks the final conflict, and therefore the end, of two forces which are the worst enemies of civil freedom, – the absolute monarchy, and the revolution.

THE BALANCE OF CLASSES
ALBERT VENN DICEY*

'It is the principle of the English Constitution, that parliament should be a mirror,– a representation of every class; not according to heads, not according to numbers, but according to everything which gives weight and importance in the world without; so that the various classes of this country may be heard, and their views expressed fairly in the House of Commons, without the possibility of any one class outnumbering or reducing to silence all the other classes in the kingdom.'[1]

In these words Sir Hugh Cairns[a] sums up that theory of representation, which makes it the end of Parliament to be the representative of classes. This view is entertained by persons who differ in every other political opinion. It is the pet theory of so-called philosophic Liberals, and of most intelligent Conservatives. Nothing indeed can show its prevalence more clearly than the indignant criticism excited by expressions of Mr. Gladstone, which seemed, though in all probability untruly, to intimate his adhesion to a totally different doctrine. For it cannot be concealed that the theory of class representation is fundamentally opposed to the arguments, which, till recently, have been employed by all democratic or radical Reformers. Of such men, Mr. Bright is the most eminent, as well as the most consistent leader; and the idea which lies at the bottom of all his theories of Reform, is, that

---

*   A. V. Dicey. 'The Balance of Classes', *Essays on Reform* (London: Macmillan, 1867), pp. 67–84.
[1]   Speech, April, 1866, Hansard, p. 1463.
[a]   Sir Hugh McCalmont Cairns (1819–85), first Earl Cairns. Active in opposing the Second Reform Act in the House of Lords. Appointed Lord-Chancellor by Disraeli in 1878.

representation should be primarily a representation of persons – only in so far as it may be so accidentally, a representation of classes. It is because of his entertaining this belief, a belief shared by nearly all the older Liberal leaders, that he is constantly reproached with the crudeness and unphilosophic character of his policy; and the fact becomes every day more apparent, that between persons who hold that the object of Reform is more nearly to represent classes, and those who cling to the opinion that its main end is gradually to give the full rights of citizens to all persons, there can be no ultimate agreement as to the course which ought to be pursued by Parliamentary Reformers. It is, therefore, of primary importance for all Liberals to make up their minds whether Parliament ought or ought not to aim at being, in the words of Sir Hugh Cairns, 'a mirror of every class;' or whether it should aim to represent persons, and leave the representation of classes to take care of itself.

Before entering upon a discussion of the class theory of representation, and the arguments by which it is supported, it is well to clear away some misconceptions by which that discussion is confused. It is often, for example, asserted, that the most desirable kind of Reform is one which should admit the working classes to a share of influence, without changing the balance of power. Persons who use this language either do not understand what their words mean, or mean something which they do not wish their hearers to understand; for it is of the very essence of all Reform to change the balance of power. If the working classes gain influence, some other class must lose it; and if each class remains with no more political power than before, then there will have been no real Reform; and it is not to be supposed that either working men or any other class, will be satisfied with a measure, simply because it is entitled a Reform Bill, and because, while changing nothing, it professes to change everything. If, on the other hand, what is intended is, that the alteration to be desired is one which shall leave the rich as powerful as now, but effect some new distribution of power between the 10*l.* householders and the working men, then the wish expressed for a Bill which does not change the balance of power, is doubly dishonest; since it does not express what it means, and seems to express what it does not mean. For the desire really felt is not that political power should remain unchanged, but that, within certain limits, it should be surreptitiously shifted in a particular direction.

It is again to be noted that much which is often and honestly said about the effects of giving representatives according to numbers, is, strictly speaking, not argument, but rhetoric. It is constantly asserted, with more or less distinctness, that the enfranchisement of the masses is the disfranchisement of the rich. Such an assertion is, however, nothing more than a rhetorical mode of saying that the influence of the rich will be unduly diminished by a wide extension of the franchise; for, as a matter of fact, no man is disfranchised by enfranchisement of another. Take the most extreme case, and suppose universal suffrage established. In this case the wealthier classes might indeed be in a minority, but they would be as far from disfranchisement as any other equal number of persons in the kingdom. Under the most unfavourable circumstances they would exercise a controlling influence by supporting that section of the people to which they were least opposed. But the influence of a minority is always considerable, and the influence of a rich minority could never be insignificant. If a proposal were made really to disfranchise all possessors, say of a thousand a year, rich men would soon perceive the difference between being disfranchised and being in a minority. One partner of a numerous firm never dreams of stating that he has no vote because he may constantly be outvoted; and expressions which would be ridiculous applied to the transactions of private life do not gain additional force or accuracy from being applied to politics. The real question at issue is not one of disfranchisement, but of supremacy. Advocates of class representation desire such a political arrangement as would enable a minority, in virtue of their education, wealth, &c. to carry out their views, even though opposed to the sentiments of the majority of the people. Democrats, on the other hand, desire the gradual establishment of a constitutional system under which, in the case of a direct conflict of opinion between a greater and a smaller number of citizens, the greater number may be able to carry out their own wishes. There are arguments to be used in favour of the views of either party; but the first requisite for weighing such arguments is to perceive clearly what is the point at issue. This point undoubtedly is, whether or not the greater number of the citizens ought to be made ultimately supreme in the affairs of the State.

The theory to which the passage quoted from Sir Hugh Cairns' speech gives expression may be summed up in the following propositions:—

(1) A nation consists of classes.

(2) Each of these may have, or may conceive themselves to have, conflicting interests.

(3) It is, therefore, desirable that each class should be duly represented.

(4) Since one of these classes greatly exceeds the others in number, it must not be represented in proportion to its numbers, because, if it were so, this class would be supreme.

This theory is supported by arguments which assume very various forms, but which may be reduced to a few heads.

It is, in the first place, urged that the nation is in reality an organization, of which classes are the essential parts; and much ingenuity is shown in the use of different metaphors, all of which aim at setting forth the idea that a nation does not primarily consist of the individuals who make it up. To most minds these attempts to distinguish between the nation and the individuals to be found in it, it will appear as idle and unsatisfactory as the Aristotelian discussions about the natural priority of the individual or the State. And without going into political metaphysics, ordinary writers may be allowed to point out that though individuals may be considered as members of different classes, it is as individuals that they either suffer or inflict wrong, and that their individual interests can by no device whatever be merged in that of the class to which they belong. The assertion indeed of a most able writer that 'John Smith *quâ* John Smith cannot be oppressed, but John Smith *quâ* artisan can', neatly sums up what will appear to most persons the exact opposite of the truth, and affords a species of *reductio ad absurdum* of the application of very doubtful metaphysics to the defence of a doubtful political dogma.

It is not, however, reasoning of a transcendental kind which has lent a weight to the theory of class representation. An argument of real force, urged by some speculators, is that the introduction into the body of members belonging to different orders of the community would tend greatly to improve the character of the legislature. No candid critic can deny that there is some truth in this allegation. The remark, however, may be justly made that representation according to numbers is not inconsistent with the presence in Parliament of men belonging to different pursuits and professions. The first French Assembly, after the Revolution of 1848, was elected by universal suffrage, yet amongst it numerous faults this was not one, that it did not contain certain members from different sections of the nations. It must further be noticed that it is not, and never has been, a primary object of constitutional arrangements to get together the best possible Parliament in point of intellectual capacity. Indeed, it would be inconsistent with the idea of a representative government to attempt to form a Parliament far superior in intelligence to the mass of the nation. There is no doubt that most country gentlemen were till recently, if they are not still, grossly ignorant of political economy, yet no one supposes that for the purposes of free government it would be desirable to exclude from Parliament every squire who could not understand the fallacies of Protection.

A remark of far more importance is, that this argument, whatever it is worth, points towards the direct representation of orders, and means that there ought to be representatives of, for example, the Church, law, medicine, the working classes, &c. seated in Parliament; and thus its value depends upon the answer given to a question hereafter to be considered, *i.e.* whether or not it be on the whole desirable that Parliament should consist of Members for orders. It will, however, be found that the demand for class representation gains its force almost exclusively from a single line of reasoning.

It is said that without class representation the interest of individuals will never be fairly protected. Each class (and the working classes may be considered in this respect neither better nor worse than the rest of the community) will always consider its own interest as supreme, and therefore if it be sovereign will oppress all other portions of the community; hence it is of infinite importance that no one class should be sovereign. But representation of numbers would make the working classes sovereign, and thus, in denying to them representation according to numbers, statesmen deny them no more than is refused to every other class.

This argument admits of profuse and effective illustration. It is said, for example, that the working men, being in a majority, might throw all the burden of taxation on the shoulders of the rich, and expend all the proceeds of taxation on the enjoyments of the poor, or might establish laws for the protection of labour as oppressive as the laws which English gentlemen established for the protection of corn.

The weakness of this argument is that the truth it contains applies to all governments. The danger pointed to in the supremacy of numbers is a danger common to all supremacy. No distribution of representatives, no cunning device of political theorists, can prevent the existence in every State of some person or body of persons who can if they choose act contrary to the interests of the rest of the community.

But if it be alleged that tyranny is specially to be feared where numbers are supreme, there seems to be little proof for the allegation. In all countries the majority must be a fluctuating, unknown, indefinite body, which has neither the will nor the power to act with systematic tyranny. In England especially, where classes are intermingled, and where it is absolutely impossible to draw a clearly marked line between the different divisions of the nation,– where, for instance, it is hard to say what are the limits of the so-called middle class,– it is highly improbable that the whole of the poor (and it is only when acting as a whole that they could in any case be supreme) would act together as one man in opposition to the wishes of all those who are not technically working men.

For the so-called working class is, like all others, notoriously broken into divisions; for example, of artisans and labourers. The legitimate influence – to use the words in their true sense – of the rich and the educated has immense weight with all who depend for their livelihood on their wages. It is, indeed, a more reasonable fear that a widely extended suffrage may unduly increase the influence of landowners and capitalists, than that it will lead to the unexampled result of placing the multitude in permanent supremacy over the rich. There is, however, no use in blinking the fact that occasions might arise on which the majority of the nation might adopt a policy opposed to the judgment of the minority. But on such occasions, it is as likely as not that the majority might be in the right. The American Union was saved because the energy and decision of artisans and farmers overruled the hesitation and weakness of the merchants of New York.[b]

But, of course, the majority is no infallible ruler. The working men of England might easily commit errors as great – they could not commit greater – as the mistakes committed by George III. and by Pitt.[c] If, however, the majority should fall into errors, it may still be well that the majority should rule. All belief in free government rests ultimately on the conviction that a people gains more by the experience, than it loses by the errors, of liberty, and it is difficult to perceive why a truth that holds good of individuals and of nations, should not apply equally to the majority of the individuals who constitute a nation.

Advocates of class representation have expended immense ingenuity in devising schemes for effecting an hypothetical balance of power, and the complexity of these devices has given an appearance of philosophic profundity to the theory which makes such devices necessary; for it is difficult for any one to believe that an object which needs thought and ingenuity for its attainment may, after all, not be worth attaining. But calm observers, though willing to give all due weight to the objections which may be urged against the representation of numbers, may yet be inclined to suspect that thinkers who advocate the establishment of a balance of power, entertain views open to greater difficulties than are the theories which these thinkers assail. It is, at any rate, worth while to remember that a scheme may be philosophic, even though it be simple, and though it command the support of Mr. Bright.

[b] In the election of 1860 the Republican candidate, Abraham Lincoln, carried every county in New England and much of the North West. However, while he carried most of New York State, the area around New York City voted heavily for Democrat and Constitutional Union candidates.

[c] William Pitt, first Earl of Chatham, 1708–78. The 'errors' refer to the vain efforts of Pitt and the king to secure the British empire in North America and their refusal to acknowledge American Independence.

All schemes for effecting a so-called balance of classes are open to a primary charge of utter impracticability. Their object is to give 'due' weight to each interest, but no standard exists by which 'due' weight may be measured. Mr. Disraeli is honestly convinced that the landed interest has not its due share of power. Most other persons would think a diminution of the influence of the country gentlemen essential to the establishment of a fair constitutional balance; but there exists no test by which to decide between the correctness of Mr. Disraeli's views and the views of his opponents, unless principles be introduced which are fatal to the theory of the balance of power. Sir Hugh Cairns with his usual acuteness, perceives this difficulty, and gets over it by the suggestion that each class should have the power in Parliament which it has in the world without. Unluckily, the very object of all sincere Reformers is to effect a change in the social and other influences of different portions of society. It is, therefore, idle to hope to satisfy the demand for Reform by creating a Parliament, the object of which is permanently to embody distinctions, which Reformers desire to diminish.[2]

But even were it possible that persons of opposite views, such as Mr. Mill and Mr. Disraeli, could be brought to agree on the exact proportion of influence which ought to be retained by the landed, commercial, and working classes, under a future constitutional arrangement, such an agreement would be as worthless as it would be illusory; for in politics nothing is more

---

[2]   It is not in truth to be supposed that a skilled lawyer, well accustomed to practical life, intends deliberately to advocate any elaborate arrangement for a representation of different classes. He would, doubtless, be content with the existing state of things. What, however, he must be taken to urge is, that any change ought to have as its object the giving representation in accordance with the power of different classes out of Parliament. And the policy he proposes may be easily shown to be open to the objection that has been brought against it. The landowners or capitalists, for example, have immense influence in modern society. Landowners and capitalists ought, therefore, according to Sir Hugh Cairns, to have an immense share of the representation. If this share be given them they will indubitably have the power, which they are likely to use, of hindering changes which might affect their own weight in society. Hence, deliberately to give to landowners and capitalists representation according to their influence is to perpetuate and, as it were, stereotype that influence.

certain than that it is impossible to predict how political and social forces will adjust themselves under a new Constitution. In 1832, no prophet could have foretold, as the result of the Reform Bill, that the practical supremacy of the middle classes would have been found compatible with government through the nobility.[d] Had it been deemed requisite to ascertain beforehand what would be the exact amount of weight given by the Reform Act to each section of society, Gatton and Old Sarum[e] might still be sending up members to parliament, whilst Commission after Commission was attempting to obtain information, which is absolutely essential if it be desirable to establish an elaborate balance of power, and yet is in its own nature unattainable.

Theoretical speculators easily perform in imagination feats which are found impossible by practical politicians, and various enthusiasts have sketched out, with more or less ingenuity and inconsistency, what should be the exact balance of power established in what one of their number has termed 'the Constitution of the Future'.[f] Whoever wishes to see an excellent specimen of the speculations of the men who are called 'thinkers', should read with care Professor Lorimer's book, in which this Constitution of the future is sketched out. It

---

[d] 'For a generation after the Reform Bill, the benches on both sides of the House were still occupied by country gentlemen...But many of the country gentlemen, especially on the Whig side, had been chosen by the votes of the Ten Pound citizens. The trial of strength between the Ten Pound householders and the landlord interest, came in the 'forties over the issue of the Corn Laws.' G. M. Macaulay, *British History in the Nineteenth Century* (London: Longmans, 1922), p. 241.

[e] In 1830, the Borough of Gatton returned two Members of Parliament by an electorate of two. In Old Sarum, seven electors returned two Members.

[f] Professor James Lorimer (1818–90). Appointed to the Regius Chair of Public Law at the University of Edinburgh in 1865. Author of *Political Progress not Necessarily Democratic: or Relative Equality the True Foundation of Liberty* (1857). (This work formed one of the subjects of John Stuart Mill's article for *Fraser's Magazine* (1859) entitled 'Recent Writers on Reform'. Although Mill agreed with Lorimer's proposal to introduce universal but unequal suffrage, he maintained that education rather than 'social influence' should be the criterion by which votes should be weighted.) Lorimer was also the author of *Constitutionalism of the Future: or Parliament the Mirror of the Nation* (1865) – a book dedicated to Mill.

is instructive, at any rate, to observe that a Professor and a thinker, quite consistently with his theory, while giving votes to every man in proportion to his merits, gives only one vote to a simple citizen and ten votes to the happy possessor of ten thousand a year, who, indeed, would, under the Professor's scheme, as a general rule, have at least twenty votes.[3] This is instructive, because it points to the conclusion that the principles laid down by Sir High Cairns almost inevitably tend in practice, as they do in Professor Lorimer's theory, to the establishment of a Plutocracy. But even this theory does not fully exhibit one of the most important features of class representation.

This feature is the introduction into Parliament of the representatives of orders. The ablest and most sagacious of the advocates of class representation distinctly contemplate this result, and, as before pointed out, one of the strongest arguments in favour of their theory is the advantage which it is supposed would accrue to the country from the presence in the legislature of the members of different classes or orders. It is indeed a boast of some able writers that, if they deny to the working classes representation in proportion to their numbers, they are willing to ensure the working classes the possession of a certain body of, say fifty or a hundred, special representatives of the masses. It is in truth so apparent that any theory of class representation must ultimately lead to the presence in Parliament of members specially delegated to represent such different classes, that it becomes a matter of importance in estimating that theory, to settle whether the presence of such members would be a national gain or loss. The presence in Parliament of fifty or a hundred working men, or at any rate distinct representatives of working men, would not, it must be owned, in all points of view be without advantage. But if these men sat as the special representatives of a class, the advantage which their presence might confer would be purchased by incalculable evils. It may be pointed out in passing, that representation by orders, after having been tried in all European countries, has been universally given up, and this fact

---

[3]   Constitution of the Future, p. 174.

of itself suggests that such representation has peculiar defects; but the special evil which at the present moment needs attention is that the proposed representation of orders threatens to introduce supremacy of numbers in its worst form. Let there, for example, be fifty special representatives of working men in Parliament, and these fifty men will inevitably become, not members, but tribunes. Elected by a class numerically the greatest, they will soon claim and exert an authority beyond that given them by their numbers. On a question of peace or war, they would have it in their power to enter, on behalf of the mass of the nation, protests against the course adopted by the majority in Parliament, and such protests could not in practice go unheeded whatever might be the theory of the Constitution.

In this matter it is unnecessary to appeal to *à priori* reasoning. Irish and Scotch Members are from the necessity of the case representatives of a class, and do, therefore, exert a force out of all proportion to their numbers. Few governments would dare to legislate for Scotland or Ireland in the face of the united opposition of the Scotch or Irish Members. Any one who is unwilling to see the working classes legislate for the majority of the nation, as the Scotch Members legislate for Scotland, will prefer the direct supremacy of numbers to the indirect supremacy of a tribunate.

For class representatives have an inherent defect beyond that of exerting undue influence. From their very position they at once display and intensify class feeling. What the leaders of Convocation are to the body of the clergy, that the specially elected leaders of the working men would be to the artisans. They would be the most fanatical, the most narrow of their class. Our country representatives, again, are a near approach to the representatives of a class; and the country gentlemen all but hooted down Mr. Mill because he tried to make them understand that a sick cow ought not to be valued at the price of a healthy animal.[g] America itself is a standing warning, not

---

g   In a Commons debate on a Bill drawn up in response to a recent cattle plague, Mill, as M. P. for Westminster, had cautioned against the award of excessive compensation for diseased cattle. He was concerned that the amount of compensation should not be so high as to induce farmers to

against the supremacy of numbers, but against artificial schemes for insuring a definite amount of power to certain classes, since the whole theory of State Rights is nothing but a theory of class rights carried out on a larger scale; and this theory till recently obtained such weight throughout America that most politicians were ready to attribute a sort of sacredness to the rights of States, just as enthusiasts for a balance of power are ready to see something sacred in the name of a class. For it is necessary to point out that, after all, there is nothing specially to be reverenced in orders or interests. Half the evils of modern England arise from the undue prominence of class distinctions, and the fundamental fault of class representation is its tendency to intensify differences which it is an object of political Reform to remove.

In critizing a theory of class representation, the words 'classes', 'orders', or 'interests', must be constantly employed. The very employment, however, of those expressions gives an undue advantage to the view criticized. For it is, after all, to be suspected that the very basis on which this view rests is not firm enough to support the conclusions grounded upon it. This basis is the assumption that English society can be, for practical purposes, divided into classes or orders. Classes no doubt exist, but they are not of the distinct, clearly-marked, homogeneous kind which the class theory of representation requires. In a society such as that of the Middle Ages, where marked orders existed, representation by orders, with all its disadvantages, arose, as it were naturally, from the surrounding condition of civilization. In a society like that of modern England it is difficult to find the orders on which laboriously to build a scheme of class representation. Take, for example, a class frequently mentioned in political discussions, that of the 10*l.* householders. What, after all, is the real community of view or interest, which binds the members of the class together? They

slaughter animals whose survival chances were good. But his speech concluded with an attack upon aristocracies who 'enjoyed the highest honours and advantages' but were unwilling 'to bear the first brunt of the inconveniences and evils which fell upon the country generally'. Viscount Cranbourne led a vigorous defence of the agricultural interest as the national interest against Mill. *Hansard's Parliamentary Debates,* IIIrd series, CLXXXI, 14 February 1866, pp. 460–502.

are of different politics; they pursue different professions; they belong, in many cases, to different religious bodies. Looked at in one point of view, they may be called a class; looked at in another, they are a disconnected mass of different small classes. Take, again, any class of Englishmen, from the highest to the lowest, and it will be found to mix, by imperceptible degrees, with the class below it. Who can say where the upper class ends, or where the middle class begins? Who, again, can draw a line which shall accurately divide working men from small tradesmen? Yet if there exist a class or order, it is the class of workmen. To those who see this class from without, and from a distance, it appears, no doubt, much more of a class or order than it really is; because its subdivisions escape notice. That these exist is granted even by Conservative speakers, who, like Sir Hugh Cairns, injure the force of their arguments by indulging in boasts of the Conservatism to be found amongst artisans. But let it be fairly granted that there is more class feeling among workmen than amongst the rest of the community. The reason is not far to seek. Treated as a class, they have fallen back upon their class feeling, and have devoted their energies to class interests. If it had not been for the Reform of 1832, the middle classes would form as distinct a body as the working men. A free extension of the franchise in 1867 will, in thirty years, make the artisans as little distinguishable from the rest of the nation as are the men whose fathers in 1832 almost overthrew the Constitution from which they were excluded.

Much indeed has been said and written by Professors and theorists as to the unphilosophic character of the Democratic view of Reform. This view is, however, as a fact, held by men who, whether they think rightly or wrongly, have as much right to the much abused name of 'thinkers' as their opponents. The so-called unphilosophic and vulgar Radicalism, with which politicians are taunted, who desire, slowly but ultimately, to make the majority of the nation arbiter of the nation's destiny, rests upon two principles: the first, that on the whole each man is the best manager of his own affairs; the second, that citizens ought to be looked upon, primarily, as persons, secondarily only, as members of classes. Those who take this view need not be blind to the advantages which may be gained by the free representation in Parliament of different portions of society. But they hold that, as a matter of fact, such representation of classes as is desirable has been obtained by gradually extending the suffrage to those personally fitted for its exercise, without measuring beforehand what might be the exact influence of such extension on the balance of power. It is, moreover, in the opinion of such radical Reformers, worth incurring some risk, to bring the mass of the nation within the bounds of the Constitution. The widest franchise any government is likely to propose, would, after all, stop far short of universal suffrage. The question, after all, therefore is, whether the risk (if risk it be) be not worth running. The theory of class representation rests, indeed, on the assumption that theorists can sketch out the future of the nation; but this is an assumption which history and experience emphatically contradict. It rests on the further assumption, that national progress is best attained by ingeniously balancing class against class, and selfish interest against selfish interest. This assumption is, indeed, expressed by Sir Hugh Cairns, in a form which, from its very vagueness, commands general assent. Most persons are captivated by the idea of Parliament being a mirror of the nation; but a speaker's meaning must be gathered as much at least from the circumstances under which he speaks, as from his mere words. The true interpretation of Sir Hugh Cairns' sentiments is to be found in the fact, that his speech was made in opposition to a proposal, not for universal suffrage, but for a very moderate extension of the franchise, and that his political friends have averred, that if Parliament is to be a perfect 'mirror', it should represent, at least as fully as at present, the important class of landowners.

LIBERAL LEGISLATION AND FREEDOM OF CONTRACT
T. H. GREEN[*]

That a discussion on this subject is opportune will hardly be disputed by any one who noticed the line of argument by which at least two of the Liberal measures of last session were opposed. To the Ground Game Act[a] it was objected that it interfered with freedom of contract between landlord and tenant. It withdrew the sanction of law from any agreement by which the occupier of land should transfer to the owner the exclusive right of killing hares and rabbits on the land in his occupation. The Employers' Liability Act[b] was objected to on similar grounds. It did not indeed go the length of preventing masters and workmen from contracting themselves out of its operation. But it was urged that it went on the wrong principle of encouraging the workman to look to the law for the protection which he ought to secure for himself by voluntary contract. 'The workman', it was argued, 'should be left to take care of himself by the terms of his agreement with the employer. It is not for the State to step in and say, as by the new act it says, that when a workman is hurt in carrying out the instructions of the employer or his foreman, the employer, in the absence of a special agreement to the contrary, shall be liable for compensation. If the law thus takes to protecting men, whether tenant-farmers, or pitmen, or railway servants, who ought to be able to protect themselves, it tends to weaken

---

[*] T. H. Green, *Liberal Legislation and Freedom of Contract* (London: Slatter & Rose. 1881), pp. 5–22.

[a] Ground Game Act 1880.

[b] Employers Liability Act 1880.

111

their self-reliance, and thus in unwisely seeking to do them good, it lowers them in the scale of moral beings.'

Such is the language which was everywhere in the air last summer, and which many of us, without being convinced by it, may have found it difficult to answer. The same line of objection is equally applicable to other legislation of recent years – to our Factory Acts, Education Acts, and laws relating to public health. They all, in one direction or another, limit a man's power of doing what he will with what he considers his own. They all involve the legal prohibition of certain agreements between man and man, and as there is nothing to force men into these agreements, it might be argued that, supposing them to be mischievous, men would, in their own interest, gradually learn to refuse them. There is other legislation which the Liberal party is likely to demand, and which is sure to be objected to on the same ground – with what justice we shall see as we proceed. If it is proposed to give the Irish tenant some security in his holding, to save him from rack-renting and from the confiscation of the results of his labour in the improvement of the soil, it will be objected that in so doing the State goes out of its way to interfere with the contracts, possibly beneficial to both sides, which landlord and tenant would otherwise make with each other. Leave the tenant, it will be said, to secure himself by contract. Meanwhile the demand for greater security of tenure is growing stronger amongst our English farmers, and should it be proposed – as it must before this Parliament expires – to give legal effect to it, the proposal will be met by the same cry, that it is an interference with the freedom of contract – unless, indeed, like Lord Beaconsfield's Act of 1875, it undoes with one hand what it professes to do with the other.[c]

There are two other matters with which the Liberal leaders have virtually promised to deal, and upon which they are sure to be met by an appeal to the supposed inherent right of every man to do what he will with his own. One is the present system of settling land, the other the liquor traffic. The only effectual reform of the Land Laws is to put a stop to those settlements or bequests by which at present a landlord may prevent a

[c]   Agricultural Holdings Act, 1875.

successor from either converting any part of his land into money or from dividing it among his children. But if it is proposed to take away from the landlord this power of hampering prosperity, it will be said to be an interference with his free disposal of his property. As for the liquor traffic, it is obvious that even the present Licensing Laws, ineffectual as some of us think them, interfere with the free sale of an article in large consumption, and that with the concession of 'local option' the interference would, to say the least, be probably carried much further. I have said enough to show that the most pressing political questions of our time are questions of which the settlement, I do not say necessarily involves an interference with freedom of contract, but is sure to be resisted in the sacred name of individual liberty, not only by all those who are interested in keeping things as they are but by others to whom freedom is dear for its own sake, and who do not sufficiently consider the conditions of its maintenance in such a society as ours. In this respect there is a noticeable difference between the present position of political reformers and that in which they stood a generation ago. Then they fought the fight of reform in the name of individual freedom against class privilege. Their opponents could not with any plausibility invoke the same name against them. Now, in appearance – though, as I shall try to show, not in reality – the case is changed. The nature of the genuine political reformer is perhaps always the same. The passion for improving mankind, in its ultimate object, does not vary. But the immediate object of reformers, and the forms of persuasion by which they seek to advance them, vary much in different generations. To a hasty observer they might even seem contradictory, and to justify the notion that nothing better than a desire for change, selfish or perverse, is at the bottom of all reforming movements, Only those who will think a little longer about it can discern the same old cause of social good against class interests, for which, under altered names, Liberals are fighting now as they were fifty years ago.

Our political history since the first reform Act naturally falls into three divisions. The first, beginning with the reform of Parliament, and extending to Sir R. Peel's administration,[d] is

---

[d]   1841–46.

marked by the struggle of free society against close privileged corporations. Its greatest achievement was the establishment of representative municipal governments in place of the close bodies which had previously administered the affairs of our cities and boroughs[e] – a work which after an interval of nearly half a century we hope shortly to see extended to the rural districts.[f] Another important work was the overhauling the immense charities of the country, and the placing them under something like adequate public control.[g] And the natural complement of this was the removal of the grosser abuses in the administration of the Church – the abolition of pluralities and sinecures, and the reform of cathedral chapters.[h] In all this, while there was much that contributed to the freedom of our civil life, there was nothing that could possibly be construed as an interference with the rights of the individual. No one was disturbed in doing what he would with his own. Even those who had fattened on abuses had their vested interests duly respected, for the House of Commons then as now had 'quite a passion for compensation.' With the Ministry of Sir R. Peel began the struggle of society against monopolies; in other words, the liberation of trade.[i] Some years later Mr. Gladstone, in his famous budgets, was able to complete the work which his master began, and it is now some twenty years since the last vestige of protection for any class of traders or producers disappeared. The taxes on knowledge,[j] as they were called, followed the taxes on food, and since most of us grew up there has been no exchangeable commodity in England except land – no doubt a large exception – of which the exchange has not been perfectly free.

The realisation of compete freedom of contract was the special object of this reforming work. It was to set men at liberty to dispose of what they had made their own that the free-trader worked. He only interfered to prevent interference. He would put restraint on no man in doing anything that did not

---

[e]   Municipal Corporations Act, 1835.
[f]   Local Government Act, 1888.
[g]   Charity Commissioners Act, 1853.
[h]   The Pluralities Bill, 1838; Ecclesiastical Duties and Revenues Act, 1840.
[i]   Repeal of the Corn Laws, 1846.
[j]   The advertisement duty was repealed in 1853. In 1855 the compulsory newspaper stamp was abolished. In 1861 the paper duty was abolished.

directly check the free dealing of some one in something else. But of late reforming legislation has taken, as I have pointed out, a seemingly different direction. It has not at any rate been so readily identifiable with the work of liberation. In certain respects it has put restraints on the individual in doing what he will with his own. And it is noticeable that this altered tendency begins, in the main, with the more democratic Parliament of 1868. It is true that the earlier Factory Acts, limiting as they do by law the conditions under which certain kinds of labour may be bought and sold, had been passed some time before. The first approach to an effectual Factory Act dates as far back as the time of the first Reform Act, but it only applied to the cotton industry, and was very imperfectly put in force.[k] It aimed at limiting the hours of labour for children and young persons. Gradually the limitation of hours came to be enforced, other industries were brought under the operation of the restraining laws, and the same protection extended to women as to young persons. But it was only alongside of the second Reform Act in 1867 that an attempt was made by Parliament to apply the same rule to every kind of factory and workshop;[l] only later still, in the first parliament elected partly by household suffrage, that efficient measures were taken for enforcing the restraints which previous legislation had in principle required.[m] Improvements and extensions in detail have since been introduced – largely through the influence of Mr. Mundella[n] – and now we have a system of law by which in all our chief industries except the agricultural, the employment of children except as half-timers is effectually prevented, the employment of women and young persons is effectually restricted to ten hours a day, and in all places of employment

[k]   Act to regulate the Labour of Children and Young Persons in Mills and Factories, 1833.

[l]   The Factory Acts Extension and Workshops Regulation Act, 1867.

[m]   In 1871 the administration of the Workshops Act (which applied to premises employing less than fifty persons) was passed to the Factory Inspectorate.

[n]   Anthony John Mundella (1825–97); Educationalist, Liberal M.P. and President of the Board of Trade, 1886 and 1892–94. His Education Act of 1880 made compulsory the school attendance of children under thirteen.

health and bodily safety have all the protection which rules can given them.[o]

If factory regulation had been attempted, though only in a piecemeal way, some time before we had a democratic House of Commons, the same cannot be said of educational law. It was the parliament elected by a more popular suffrage in 1868 that passed, as we know, the first great Education Act. That act introduced compulsory schooling. It left the compulsion, indeed, optional with local School Boards, but compulsion is the same in principle – is just as much compulsion by the State – whether exercised by the central Government or delegated by that Government to provincial authorities. The Education Act of 1870 was a wholly new departure in English legislation, though Mr. Forster [p] was wise enough to proceed tentatively, and leave the adoption of compulsory bye-laws to the discretion of School Boards. It was so just as much as if he had attempted at once to enforce compulsory attendance through the action of the central Government. The principle was established once for all that parents were not to be allowed to do as they willed with their children, if they willed either to set them to work or to let them run wild without elementary education. Freedom of contract in respect of all dealings with the labour of children was so far limited.

I need not trouble you with recalling the steps by which the principle of the act of 1870 has since been further applied and enforced. It is evident that in the body of school and factory legislation which I have noticed we have a great system of interference with freedom of contract. The hirer of labour is prevented from hiring it on terms to which the person of whom he hires it could for the most part have been readily brought to agree. If children and young persons and women were not ready in many cases, either from their own wish, or under the influence of parents and husbands, to accept employment of the kind which the law prohibits, there would have been no occasion for the prohibition. It is true that adult men are not placed directly under the same restriction. The law does not forbid them from working as long hours as they please. But I

---

[o]   Factory and Workshops' Consolidating Act, 1878.
[p]   William Edward Forster (1818–86), Liberal statesman who laid the basis of a national system of education in his 1870 Education Act.

need not point out here that in effect the prevention of the employment of juvenile labour beyond certain hours, amounts, at least in the textile industries, to the prevention of the working of machinery beyond those hours. It thus indirectly puts a limit on the number of hours during which the manufacturer can employ his men. And if it is only accidentally, so to speak, that the hiring of men's labour is interfered with by the half-time and ten hours' system, the interference on grounds of health and safety is as direct as possible. The most mature man is prohibited by law from contracting to labour in factories, or pits, or workshops, unless certain rules for the protection of health and limb are complied with. In like manner he is prohibited from living in a house which the sanitary inspector pronounces unwholesome. The free sale or letting of a certain kind of commodity is thereby prevented. Here, then, is a great system of restriction, which yet hardly any impartial person wishes to see reversed; which many of us wish to see made more complete. Perhaps, however, we have never thoroughly considered the principles on which we approve it. It may be well, therefore, to spend a short time in ascertaining those principles. We shall then be on surer ground in approaching those more difficult questions of legislation which must shortly be dealt with, and of which the settlement is sure to be resisted in the name of individual liberty.

We shall probably all agree that freedom, rightly understood, is the greatest of blessings – that its attainment is the true end of all our effort as citizens. But when we thus speak of freedom, we should consider carefully what we mean by it. We do not mean merely freedom from restraint or compulsion. We do not mean merely freedom to do as we like irrespectively of what it is that we like. We do not mean a freedom that can be enjoyed by one man or one set of men at the cost of a loss of freedom to others. When we speak of freedom as something to be so highly prized, we mean a positive power or capacity of doing or enjoying something worth doing or enjoying, and that, too, something that we do or enjoy in common with others. We mean by it a power which each man exercises through the help or security given him by his fellow-men, and which he in turn helps to secure for them. When we measure the progress of a society by its growth in freedom, we measure it by the increasing development and exercise on the whole of those powers of contributing to social good with which we believe the members of the society to be endowed – in short, by the greater power on the part of the citizens as a body to make the most and best of themselves. Thus, though of course there can be no freedom among men who act not willingly, but under compulsion, yet on the other hand the mere removal of compulsion, the mere enabling a man to do as he likes is in itself no contribution to true freedom. In one sense no man is so well able to do as he likes as the wandering savage. He has no master. There is no one to say him nay. Yet we do not count him really free, because the freedom of savagery is not strength, but weakness. The actual powers of the noblest savage do not admit of comparison with those of the humblest citizen of a law-abiding state. He is not the slave of man, but he is the slave of nature. Of compulsion by natural necessity he has plenty of experience, though of restraint by society none at all. Nor can he deliver himself from that compulsion except by submitting to this restrain. So to submit is the first step in true freedom, because the first step towards the full exercise of the faculties with which man is endowed. But we rightly refuse to recognise the highest development on the part of an exceptional individual or exceptional class, as an advance towards the true freedom of man, if it is founded on a refusal of the same opportunity to other men. The powers of the human mind have probably never attained such force and keenness – the proof of what society can do for the individual has never been so strikingly exhibited – as among the small groups of men who possessed civil privileges in the small republics of antiquity. The whole framework of our political ideas, to say nothing of our philosophy, is derived from them. But in them this extraordinary efflorescence of the privileged class was accompanied by the slavery of the multitude. That slavery was the condition on which it depended, and for that reason it was doomed to decay. There is no clearer ordinance of that supreme reason, often dark to us, which governs the course of man's affairs, than that no body of men should in the long run be able to strengthen itself at the cost of others' weakness. The civilisation and freedom of the ancient world were short-lived because they were partial and exceptional. If the ideal of true freedom is the maximum of power for all members of human society alike to make the best of themselves, we are right in refusing to ascribe the glory of freedom to a state in which the apparent elevation of the few is founded on the degradation of the many, and in ranking modern society, founded as it is on free industry, with all its confusion and ignorant license and waste of effort, above the most splendid of ancient republics.

If I have given a true account of that freedom which forms the goal of social effort, we shall see that freedom of contract – freedom in all the forms of doing what one will with one's own – is valuable only as a means to an end. That end is what I call freedom in the positive sense: in other words, the liberation of the powers of all men equally for contribution to a common good. No one has a right to do what he will with his own in such a way as to contravene this end. It is only through the guarantee which society gives him that he has property at all or, strictly speaking, any right to his possessions. This guarantee is founded on a sense of common interest. Every one has an interest in securing to every one else the free use and enjoyment and disposal of his possessions, so long as that freedom on the part of one does not interfere with a like freedom on the part of others, because such freedom contributes to that equal development of the faculties of all which is the highest good for all. This is the true and the only justification of rights of property. Rights of property, however, have been and are claimed which cannot be thus justified. We are all now agreed that men cannot rightly be the property of men. The institution of property being only justifiable as a means to the free exercise of the social capabilities of all, there can be no true right to property of a kind which debars one class of men from such free exercise altogether. We condemn slavery no less when it arises out of a voluntary agreement on the part of the enslaved person. A contract by which any one agreed for a certain consideration to become the slave of another we should reckon a void contract. Here, then, is a limitation upon freedom of contract which we all recognise as rightful. No contract is valid in which human persons, willingly or unwillingly, are dealt with as commodities, because such contracts of necessity defeat the end for which alone society enforces contracts at all.

Are there no other contracts which, less obviously perhaps but really, are open to the same objection? In the first place, let us consider contracts affecting labour. Labour, the economist tells us, is a commodity exchangeable like other commodities. This is in a certain sense true, but it is a commodity which attaches in a peculiar manner to the person of man. Hence restrictions may need to be placed on the sale of this commodity which would be unnecessary in other cases in order to prevent labour from being sold under conditions which make it impossible for the person selling it ever to become a free contributor to social good in any form. This is most plainly the case when a man bargains to work under conditions fatal to health, *e.g.* in an unventilated factory. Every injury to the health of the individual is, so far as it goes, a public injury. It is an impediment to the general freedom; so much deduction from our power, as members of society, to make the best of ourselves. Society is, therefore, plainly within its right when it limits freedom of contract for the sale of labour, so far as is done by our laws for the sanitary regulations of factories, workshops, and mines. It is equally within its right in prohibiting the labour of women and young persons beyond certain hours. If they work beyond those hours, the result is demonstrably physical deterioration; which, as demonstrably, carries with it a lowering of the moral forces of society. For the sake of that general freedom of its members to make the best of themselves, which it is the object of civil society to secure, a prohibition should be put by law, which is the deliberate voice of society, on all such contracts of service as in a general way yield such a result. The purchase or hire of unwholesome dwellings is properly forbidden on the same principle. Its application to compulsory education may not be quite so obvious but it will appear on a little reflection. Without a command of certain elementary arts and knowledge, the individual in modern society is as effectually crippled as by the loss of a limb or a broken constitution. He is not free to develope [*sic.*] his faculties. With a view to securing such freedom among its members it is as certainly within the province of the State to prevent children from growing up in that kind of ignorance which practically excludes them from a free career in life, as it is within its province to require the sort of building and drainage necessary for public health.

Our modern legislation then with reference to labour and education, and health – involving as it does manifold interference with freedom of contract – is justified on the ground that it is the business of the State – not indeed directly to promote moral goodness, for that, from the very nature of moral goodness, it cannot do – but to maintain the conditions without which a free exercise of the human facilities is impossible. It does not indeed follow that it is advisable for the State to do all which it is justified in doing. We are often warned now-a-days against the danger of over-legislation; or as I heard it put in a speech of the present Home Secretary [q] in days when he was sowing his political wild oats, of 'grand-motherly government.' There may be good ground for the warning, but at any rate we should be quite clear what we mean by it. The outcry against State interference is often raised by men whose real objection is not to State interference but to centralization – to the constant aggression of the central executive upon local authorities. As I have already pointed out, compulsion at the discretion of some elected municipal board, proceeds just as much from the State as does compulsion exercised by a Government office in London. No doubt, much needless friction is avoided, much is gained in the way of elasticity and adjustment to circumstances, by the independent local administration of general laws; and most of us would agree that of late there has been a dangerous tendency to override municipal discretion by the hard and fast rules of London 'departments'. But centralization is one thing: over-legislation, or the improper exercise of the power of the State, quite another. It is one question whether of late the Central Government has been unduly trenching on local government, and another question whether the law of the State, either as administered by central or by provincial authorities, has been

[q] Sir William Vernon Harcourt (1827–1904); Home Secretary, 1880–85, Leader of the Liberal Party, 1896–98. An opportunist who abandoned his opposition to temperance legislation when it seemed in his Party's interest to support it; likewise a single graduated estate duty, which he introduced as Chancellor of the Exchequer in 1894.

unduly interfering with the discretion of individuals. We may object most strongly to advancing centralization, and yet wish that the law should put rather more than less restraint on those liberties of the individual which are a social nuisance. But there are some political speculators whose objection is not merely to centralization, but to the extended action of law altogether. They think that the individual ought to be left much more to himself than has of late been the case. Might not our people, they ask, have been trusted to learn in time for themselves to eschew unhealthy dwellings, to refuse dangerous and degrading employment, to get their children the schooling necessary for making their way in the world? Would they not for their own comfort, if not from more chivalrous feeling, keep their wives and daughters from overwork? Or, failing this, ought not women, like men, to learn to protect themselves? Might not all the rules, in short, which legislation of the kind we have been discussing is intended to attain, have been attained without it; not so quickly, perhaps, but without tampering so dangerously with the independence and self-reliance of the people?

Now, we shall probably all agree that a society in which the public health was duly protected, and necessary education duly provided for, by the spontaneous action of individuals, was in a higher condition than one in which the compulsion of law was needed to secure these ends. But we must take men as we find them. Until such a condition of society is reached it is the business of the State to take the best security it can for the young citizens growing up in such health and with so much knowledge as is necessary for their real freedom. In so doing it need not at all interfere with the independence and self-reliance of those whom it requires to do what they would otherwise do for themselves. The man who, of his own right feeling, saves his wife from overwork and sends his children to school, suffers no moral degradation from a law which, if he did not do this for himself, would seek to make him do it. Such a man does not feel the law as constraint at all. To him it is simply a powerful friend. It gives him security for that being done efficiently which, with the best wishes, he might have much trouble in getting done efficiently if left to himself. No doubt it relieves him from some of the responsibility which would otherwise fall to him as head of a family, but, if he is what we are supposing him to be, in proportion as he is relieved of responsibilities in one direction he will assume them in another. The security which the State gives him for the safe housing and sufficient schooling for his family will only make him the more careful for their well-being in other respects, which he is left to look after for himself. We need have no fear, then, of such legislation having an ill-effect on those who, without the law, would have seen to that being done, though probably less efficiently, which the law requires to be done. But it was not their case that the laws we are considering were especially meant to meet. It was the overworked women, the ill-housed and untaught families for whose benefit they were intended. And the question is whether without these laws the suffering classes could have been delivered quickly or slowly from the condition they were in. Could the enlightened self-interest or benevolence of individuals, working under a system of unlimited freedom of contract, have ever brought them into a state compatible with the free development of the human faculties? No one considering the facts can have any doubt as to the answer to this question. Left to itself, or to the operation of casual benevolence, a degraded population perpetuates and increases itself. Read any of the authorised accounts, given before Royal or Parliamentary Commissions, of the state of the labourers, especially of the women and children, as they were in our great industries before the law was first brought to bear on them, and before freedom of contract was first interfered with in them. Ask yourself what chance there was of a generation, inborn and bred under such conditions, ever contracting itself out of them. Given a certain standard of moral and material well-being, people may be trusted not to sell their labour, or the labour of their children, on terms which would not allow that standard to be maintained. But with large masses of our population, until the laws we have been considering took effect, there was no such standard. There was nothing on their part, in the way either of self-respect or established demand for comforts, to prevent them from working and living, or from putting their children to work and live, in a way in which no one who is to be a healthy and free citizen can work and live. No doubt there were many high-minded employers who did their best for their work-people before the days of State-interference, but they could not prevent less scrupulous hirers of labour from hiring it on the cheapest terms. It is true that cheap labour is in the long run dear labour, but it is so only in the long run, and eager traders do not think of the long run. If labour is to be had under conditions incompatible with the health or decent housing or education of the labourer, there will always be plenty of people to buy it under those conditions, careless of the burden in the shape of rates and taxes which they may be laying up for posterity. Either the standard of well-being on the part of the sellers of labour must prevent them from selling their labour under those conditions, or the law must prevent it. With a population such as ours was forty years ago, and still largely is, the law must prevent it and continue the prevention for some generations, before the sellers will be in a state to prevent it for themselves.

As there is practically no danger of a reversal of our factory and school laws, it may seem needless to dwell at such length on their justification. I do so for two reasons – partly to remind the younger generation of citizens of the great blessing which they inherited in those laws and of the interest which they still have in their completion and extension; but still more in order to obtain some clear principles for our guidance when we approach those difficult questions of the immediate future – the questions of the Land Law and the Liquor Law.

I pointed out just now that, though labour might be reckoned an exchangeable commodity, it differed from all other commodities, inasmuch as it was inseparable from the person of the labourer. Land, too, has its characteristics, which distinguish it from ordinary commodities. It is from the land, or through the land, that the raw material of all wealth is obtained. It is only upon the land that we can live; only across the land that we can move from place to place. The State therefore, in the interest of that public freedom which it is its business to maintain, cannot allow the individual to deal as he likes with his land to the same extent to which it allows him to deal as he likes with other commodities. It is an established principle, *e.g.* that the sale of land should be enforced by law when public convenience requires it. The land owner of course gets the full value – often much more than the full value – of the land which he is compelled to sell, but of no ordinary commodity is the sale thus enforced at all. This illustrates the peculiar necessity in the public interest of putting some restraint on a man's liberty of doing what he will with his own, when it is land that he calls his own. The question is whether in the same interest further restraint does not need to be imposed on the liberty of the land-owner than is at present the case. Should not the State, which for public purposes compels the sale of land, also for public purposes prevent it from being tied up in a manner which prevents its natural distribution and keeps it in the hands of those who cannot make the most of it? At the present the greater part of the land of England is held under settlements which prevent the nominal owner from either dividing his land among his children or from selling any part of it for their benefit. It is so settled that all of it necessarily goes to the owner's eldest son. So far as any sale is allowed it must only be for the benefit of that favoured son. The evil effects of this system are two-fold. In the first place it almost entirely prevents the sale of agricultural land in small quantities and thus hinders the formation of that mainstay of social order and contentment – a class of small proprietors tilling their own land. Secondly it keeps large quantities of land in the hands of men who are too much burdened by debts or family charges to improve it. The landlord in such cases has not the money to improve, the tenant has not the security which would justify him in improving. Thus a great part of the land of England is left in a state in which, according to such eminent and impartial authorities as Lord Derby and Lord Leicester, it does not yield half of what it might. Now what is the remedy for this evil? Various palliative measures have been suggested. A very elaborate one was introduced by Lord Cairns[r] a year ago, but it fell short of the only sufficient remedy. It did not propose to prevent landlords for the future from making settlements of the kind described. It left the old power of settling land untouched on the ground that to interfere with it would be to prevent the landlord from doing what he would with his own. We urge on the contrary that this particular power on the part of the

---

[r] Earl Cairns (1819–85), Lord Chancellor in Disraeli's government in 1868, and then 1874–80. His Settled Land Bill achieved a Third Reading in the House of Lords but made little headway in the Commons.

landlord of dealing with his property – imposing, as it does, the weight of the dead hand on posterity – is against the public interest. On the simple and recognized principle that no man's land is his own for purposes incompatible with the public convenience, we ask that legal sanction should be withheld for the future from settlements which thus interfere with the distribution and improvement of land.

Such a change, though it would limit in one direction the power of dealing with land, would extend it in other directions. It would render English land on the whole a much more marketable commodity than it is at present. Its effect would be to restrain the owner of land in any one generation from putting restraints on the disposal of it in succeeding generations. It would, therefore, have the support of those Liberals who are most jealous of any interference with freedom of contract. When we come to the relations between landlord and tenant, we are on more difficult ground. It is agreed that as a general rule the more freedom of contract we have the better, with a view to that more positive freedom which consists in an open field for all men to make the best of themselves. But we must not sacrifice the end to the means. If there are certain kinds of contract for the use of land which interfere seriously with the public convenience, but which the parties immediately concerned cannot be trusted to abstain from in their own interest, such contracts should be invalid by law. It is on this ground that we justify the prohibition by the act of last Session of agreements between landlord and tenant which reserve the ground game to the landlord. If the farmers only had been concerned in the matter, they might perhaps have been left to take care of themselves. But there were public interests at stake. The country cannot afford the waste of produce and discouragement of good husbandry which result from excessive game preserving; nor can it rightly allow that wide-spread temptation to lawless habits which arise from a sort of half and half property being scattered over the country without any possibility of its being sufficiently protected. The agreements in question, therefore, were against the public interest, and as the tenant farmers themselves, from long habits of dependence, could not be trusted to refuse them, there was no alternative but to render them illegal. Perhaps as we become more alive to the evil which the Ground Game Act but partially remedied, we shall demand further legislation in the same direction, and insist that some limit be put, not merely to the landlord's power of reserving the game on land let to farmers, but to his power of keeping land out of cultivation or turning it into forest for the sake of his amusement.

But while admitting that in this matter of game, from long habit of domination on one side and dependence on the other, landlord and farmer could not safely be left to voluntary agreements, and that a special law was needed to break the back of a mischievous practice, are we to allow that in the public interest the English farmer generally needs to be restrained by law from agreements with his landlord, into which he might be induced to enter if left to himself? Is he not sufficiently enlightened as to his own interest, which is also the interest of the public, and sufficiently free in maintaining it, to refuse to take land except on conditions which will enable him to make the best of it? We may wish that he were, we may hope that some day he will be, but facts show that at present he is not. The great majority of English farmers hold their farms under the liability to be turned out without compensation at six months' or a year's notice. Now, it is certain that land connot [*sic*.] be farmed as the public interest requires that it should be except by an expenditure of capital on the part of the farmes, [*sic*.] which will not, as a general rule, be risked so long as he holds his land on these terms. It is true that, under a good landlord, the yearly tenant is as secure as if he held a long lease. But all landlords are not good, nor is a good landlord immortal. He may have a spendthrift eldest son, from whom under his settlement he cannot withhold the estate, and upon whose accession to the estate the temporary security previously enjoyed by yearly tenants will disappear. Whatever the reason, the fact remains that yearly tenancy under the present law is not sufficient to secure a due application of capital in the soil. 'The best agriculture is found on farms where tenants are protected by leases; the next best on farms where tenants are protected by the 'Lincolnshire custom';[s] the worst of all on farms whose

---

[s]   In parts of Lincolnshire in the nineteenth century, a system of 'tenant-right' operated. This gave security to tenants who had invested capital in their land by requiring the incoming tenant to compensate the outgoing

tenants are not protected at all, but rely on the honour of their landlords';* and this latter class of farms covers the greater part of England. Here, then, is proof that the majority of English farmers have either not been intelligent enough or not independent enough to insist on those contracts with their landlords which as a rule are necessary for good farming. They may in time become so, but meanwhile with the daily-increasing pressure on the means of subsistence, the country cannot afford to wait. We do not ask for any such change of the law as would hinder or discourage the farmer from making voluntary contracts with the landlord for the protection of both parties. We only wish in the public interest, which is the interest of good farming, to prevent him from taking a farm, as he now generally does, on terms incompatible with security in the outlay of capital. In the absence of leases, we wish a sufficient tenant-right to be guaranteed by law – such tenant-right as would secure to the outgoing tenant the full value of unexhausted improvements. It is only thus, we believe, that we can bring about that due cultivation of the soil which is every day becoming of greater importance to our crowded population.

This protection, which is all that can reasonably be asked for the English farmer, falls far short of that which the most impartial judges believe to be necessary for the peasant farmers in Ireland.[t] The difference between the farmers of the Irish countries may be briefly stated thus. In Ireland, far more frequently than in England, the tenant is practically not a free agent in the contract he make with his landlord. In England, during the last two or three years, the landlord has often been more afraid of losing the tenant than the tenant of losing his farm. It is comparatively easy for a man who does not succeed in getting a farm on terms under which he can make it pay to get a living in other ways. Thus in England a farmer is seldom under such pressure as to be unable to make a bargain with a

---

tenant for any unexhausted improvements. In 1852 James Caird found the custom symptomatic of a more enlightened approach to farming in the county of late, but not a direct factor in its progress. J. Caird, *English Agriculture in 1851-1852* (London: Longman, 1852), chap. 23.

* Quoted from 'English Land and English Landlords,' by the Hon. G. C. Brodrick. Cassel and Co., 1881.

t Gladstone's Land Act of 1881 set up land courts in Ireland to establish fair rents and placed other restrictions on the exclusive ownership of land.

landlord which shall be reasonably to his own advantage. In Ireland it is otherwise. The farmers there are relatively far more numerous, and, as a rule, far poorer. Nearly three-fourths of the Irish farmers (423,000 out of 596,000) hold less than 30 acres apiece; nearly half of them hold under 15 acres. A tenant on that small scale is in a very different position for bargaining with a landlord from the English farmer, as we commonly know him, with his 200 acres or more. Apart from his little farm the tenant has nothing to turn his hand to. With the exception of the linen-making in the north, Ireland has no industry but agriculture out of which a living can be made. It has been said on good authority that in many parts of Ireland eviction means starvation to the evicted tenant. This may be a strong statement, but there is no doubt that to an Irishman of the south and west (the districts at present disturbed)[u] the hiring of land to till presents itself as a necessity of life. The only alternative is emigration, and during the recent years of depression in America that alternative was to a great extent closed. Hence an excessive competition for farms, and a readiness on the part of the smaller tenants to put up with any enhancement of rent rather than relinquish their holdings. Under such conditions freedom of contract is little more than a name. The peasant farmer is scarcely more free to contract with his landlord than is a starving labourer to bargain for good wages with a master who offers him work. When many contracts between landlord and tenant are made under such pressure, reverence for contract, which is the safeguard of society, is sure to disappear, and this I believe to be the chief reason why the farmers of southern and western Ireland have been so easily led astray by the agitation of the Land League.[v] That agitation strikes at the roots of all contract, and therefore at the very foundation of modern society; but if we would effectually withstand it, we must cease to insist on maintaining the forms of free contract where the reality is impossible. We must in some way give the farmers of Ireland by law that

[u] The 'Land War', fought between 1879 and 1903, was characterised by violent struggle until 1882.
[v] The Irish Land League was formed in 1879 by Michael Davitt with the aim of overthrowing 'Landlordism'. It linked the question of land with that of Home Rule.

protection which, as a rule, they have been too weak to obtain for themselves singly by contract – protection against the confiscation of the fruits of the labour and money they have spent on the soil, whether that confiscation takes the form of actual eviction or of a constant enhancement of rent. To uphold the sanctity of contracts is doubtless a prime business of government, but it is no less its business to provide against contracts being made which from the helplessness of one of the parties to them, instead of being a security for freedom, become an instrument of disguised oppression.

I have left myself little time to speak of the principles on which some of us hold that in the matter of intoxicating drinks a further limitation of freedom of contract is needed in the interest of general freedom.[w] I say a further limitation, because there is no such thing as a free sale of these drinks at present. Men are not at liberty to buy and sell them when they will, where they will, and as they will. But our present licensing system, while it creates a class of monopolists especially interested in resisting any effectual restraint of the liquor traffic, does little to lessen the facilities for obtaining strong drink. Indeed the principle upon which licenses have been generally given has been avowedly to make it easy to get drink. The restriction of the hours of sale is no doubt a real check so far as it goes, but it remains the case that every one who has a weakness for drink has the temptation staring him in the face during all hours but those when he ought to be in bed. The effect of the present system, in short, is to prevent the drink shops from coming unpleasantly near the houses of well-to-do people, and to crowd them upon the quarters occupied by the poorer classes, who have practically no power of keeping the nuisance from them. Now it is clear that the only remedy which the law can afford for this state of things must take the form either of more stringent rules of licensing, or of a power entrusted to the householders in each district of excluding the sale of intoxicants altogether from among them.

---

[w]   The Liberal Licensing Act of 1872 set moderate limits upon the sale of alcohol and was further relaxed in an amendment by Disraeli's government in 1874. By 1880 the temperance movement was already in decline and by the early years of the twentieth century, temperance reform was no longer the spearhead of social reform.

I do not propose to discuss the comparative merits of these methods of procedure. One does not exclude the other. They may very well be combined. One may be best suited for one kind of population, the other for another kind. But either, to be effectual, must involve a large interference with the liberty of the individual to do as he likes in the matter of buying and selling alcohol. It is the justifiability of that interference that I wish briefly to consider.

We justify it on the simple ground of the recognized right on the part of society to prevent men from doing as they like, if in the exercise of their peculiar tastes, in doing as they like, they create a social nuisance. There is no right to freedom in the purchase and sale of a particular commodity, if the general result of allowing such freedom is to detract from freedom in the higher sense – from the general power of men to make the best of themselves. Now, with anyone who looks calmly at the facts there can be no doubt that the present habits of drinking in England do lay a heavy burden on the free development of man's powers for social good – a heavier burden probably than arises from all other preventable causes put together. It used to be the fashion to look on drunkenness as a vice which was the concern only of the person who fell into it, so long as it did not lead him to commit an assault on his neighbours.[x] No thoughtful man any longer looks on it this way. We know that, however decently carried on, the excessive drinking of one man means an injury to others in health, purse, and capability, to which no limits can be placed. Drunkenness in the head of a family means, as a rule, the impoverishment and degradation of all members of the family; and the presence of a drink shop at the corner of a street means, as a rule, the drunkenness of a certain number of heads of families in that street. Remove the drink shops and, as the experience of many happy communities

---

[x] In this essay *On Liberty*, J. S. Mill had written that 'Drunkenness,...in ordinary cases, is not a fit subject for legislative interference; but I should deem it perfectly legitimate that a person, who had once been convicted of any act of violence to others under the influence of drink, should be placed under a special legal restriction, personal to himself; that if he were afterwards found drunk, he should be liable to a penalty, and that if when in that state he committed another offence, the punishment to which he would be liable for that other offence should be increased in severity.' S. Collini ed., *On Liberty* (Cambridge University Press, 1989), p. 98.

sufficiently shows, you almost, perhaps in time altogether, remove drunkenness. Here, then, is a wide-spreading social evil, of which society may, if it will, by a restraining law, to a great extent, rid itself, to the infinite enhancement of the positive freedom enjoyed by its members. All that is required for the attainment of so blessed a result is so much effort and self-sacrifice on the part of the majority of citizens as is necessary for the enactment and enforcement of the restraining law. The majority of citizens may still be far from prepared for such an effort. That is a point on which I express no opinion. To attempt a restraining law in advance of the social sentiment necessary to give real effect to it, is always a mistake. But to argue that an effectual law in restraint of the drink traffic would be a wrongful interference with individual liberty, is to ignore the essential condition under which alone every particular liberty can rightly be allowed to the individual – the condition, namely, that the allowance of that liberty is not, as a rule, and on the whole, an impediment to social good.

The more reasonable opponents of the restraint for which I plead, would probably argue not so much that it was necessarily wrong in principle, as that it was one of those short cuts to a good end which ultimately defeat their own object. They would take the same line that has been taken by the opponents of state-interference in all its forms. 'Leave the people to themselves', they would say. 'As their standard of self-respect rises, as they become better housed and better educated, they will gradually shake off the evil habit. The cure so effected may not be so rapid as that brought by a repressive law, but it will be more lasting. Better that it should come more slowly through the spontaneous action of individuals than more quickly through compulsion.'

But here again we reply that it is dangerous to wait. The slower remedy might be preferable if we were sure that it was a remedy at all, but we have no such assurance. There is strong reason to think the contrary. Every year that the evil is left to itself, it becomes greater. The vested interest in the encouragement of the vice becomes larger, and the persons affected by it more numerous. If any abatement of it has already taken place, we may fairly argue that this is because it has not been altogether left to itself; for the licensing law, as it is, is much more stringent and more stringently administered than it was ten years ago. A drunken population naturally perpetuates and increases itself. Many families, it is true, keep emerging from the conditions which render them specially liable to the evil habit, but on the other hand descent through drunkenness from respectability to squalor is constantly going on. The families of drunkards do not seem to be smaller than those of sober men, though they are shorter-lived; and that the children of a drunkard should escape from drunkenness is what we call almost a miracle. Better education, better housing, more healthy rules of labour, no doubt lessen the temptations to drink for those who have the benefit of these advantages, but meanwhile drunkenness is constantly recruiting the ranks of those who cannot be really educated, who will not be better housed, who make their employments dangerous and unhealthy. An effectual liquor law in short is the necessary complement of our Factory Acts, our Education Acts, our Public Health Acts. Without it the full measure of their usefulness will never be attained. They were all opposed in their turn by the same arguments that are now used against a restraint of the facilities for drinking. Sometimes it was the argument that the State had no business to interfere with the liberties of the individual. Sometimes it was the dilatory plea that the better nature of man would in time assert itself, and that meanwhile it would be lowered by compulsion. Happily a sense of the facts and necessities of the case got the better of the delusive cry of liberty. Act after Act was passed preventing master and workman, parent and child, housebuilder and householder, from doing as they pleased, with the result of a great addition to the real freedom of society. The spirit of self-reliance and independence was not weakened by those acts. Rather it received a new development. The dead weight of ignorance and unhealthy surroundings, with which it would otherwise have had to struggle, being partially removed by law, it was more free to exert itself for higher objects. When we ask for a stringent liquor-law, which should even go to the length of allowing the householders of a district to exclude the drink traffic altogether, we are only asking for a continuation of the same work – a continuation necessary to its complete success. It is a poor sophistry to tell us that it is moral cowardice to seek to remove by law a temptation which every one ought to be able to resist for himself. It is not the part of a considerate self-reliance to remain in presence of a temptation merely for the sake of being tempted. When all temptations are removed which law can remove there will still be room enough – nay, much more room – for the play of our moral energies. The temptation to excessive drinking is one which upon sufficient evidence we hold that the law can at least greatly diminish. If it can, it ought to do so. This then, along with the effectual liberation of the soil, is the next great conquest which our democracy, on behalf of its own true freedom, has to make. The danger of legislation, either in the interests of a privileged class or for the promotion of particular religious opinions, we may fairly assume to be over. The popular jealousy of law, once justifiable enough, is therefore out of date. The citizens of England now make its law. We ask them by law to put a restraint on themselves in the matter of strong drink. We ask them further to limit – or even altogether to give up – the not very precious liberty of buying and selling alcohol, in order that they may become more free to exercise the faculties and improve the talents which God has given them.

FROM FREEDOM TO BONDAGE
HERBERT SPENCER*

Of the many ways in which common sense inferences about social affairs are flatly contradicted by events (as when measures taken to suppress a book cause increased circulation of it, or as when attempts to prevent usurious rates of interest make the terms harder for the borrower, or as when there is greater difficulty in getting things at the places of production than elsewhere) one of the most curious is the way in which the more things improve the louder become the exclamations about their badness.

In days when the people were without any political power, their subjection was rarely complained of; but after free institutions had so far advanced in England that our political arrangements were envied by continental peoples, the denunciations of aristocratic rule grew gradually stronger, until there came a great widening of the franchise, soon followed by complaints that things were going wrong for want of still further widening. If we trace up the treatment of women from the days of savagedom, when they bore all the burdens and after the men had eaten received such food as remained, up through the middle ages when they served the men at their meals, to our own when throughout our social arrangements the claims of women are always put first, we see that along with the worst treatment there went the least apparent consciousness that the treatment was bad; while now that they are better treated than ever before, the proclaiming of their grievances daily strengthens: the loudest outcries coming from 'the paradise of women', America. A century ago, when scarcely a

---

* Herbert Spencer, 'From Freedom to Bondage', in T. Mackay ed., *A Plea for Liberty: An Argument against Socialism and Socialistic Legislation* (London: John Murray, 1891), pp. 1–26.

135

man could be found who was occasionally intoxicated, and when inability to take one or two bottles of wine brought contempt, no agitation arose against the vice of drunkenness; but now that, in the course of fifty years, the voluntary efforts of temperance societies, joined with more general causes, have produced comparative sobriety, there are vociferous demands for laws to prevent the ruinous effects of the liquor traffic. Similarly again with education. A few generations back, ability to read and write was practically limited to the upper and middle classes, and the suggestion that the rudiments of culture should be given to labourers was never made, or, if made, ridiculed; but when, in the days of our grandfathers, the Sunday-school system, initiated by a few philanthropists, began to spread and was followed by the establishment of day-schools, with the result that among the masses those who could read and write were no longer the exceptions, and the demand for cheap literature rapidly increased, there began the cry that the people were perishing for lack of knowledge, and that the State must not simply educate them but must force education upon them.

And so it is, too, with the general state of the population in respect of food, clothing, shelter, and the appliances of life. Leaving out of the comparison early barbaric states, there has been a conspicuous progress from the time when most rustics lived on barley bread, rye bread, and oatmeal, down to our own time when the consumption of white wheaten bread is universal – from the days when coarse jackets reaching to the knees left the legs bare, down to the present day when labouring people, like their employers, have the whole body covered, by two or more layers of clothing – from the old era of single-roomed huts without chimneys, or from the fifteenth century when even an ordinary gentleman's house was commonly without wainscot or plaster on its walls, down to the present century when every cottage has more rooms than one and the houses of artisans usually have several, while all have fire-places, chimneys, and glazed windows, accompanied mostly by paper-hangings and painted doors; there has been, I say, a conspicuous progress in the condition of the people. And this progress has been still more marked within our own time. Any one who can look back sixty years, when the amount of pauperism was far greater than now and beggars abundant, is struck by the comparative size and finish of the new houses occupied by operatives – by the better dress of workmen, who wear broad–cloth on Sundays, and that of servant girls, who vie with their mistresses – by the higher standard of living which leads to a great demand for the best qualities of food by working people: all results of the double change to higher wages and cheaper commodities, and a distribution of taxes which has relieved the lower classes at the expense of the upper classes. He is struck, too, by the contrast between the small space which popular welfare then occupied in public attention, and the large space it now occupies, with the result that outside and inside Parliament, plans to benefit the millions form the leading topics, and every one having means is expected to join in some philanthropic effort. Yet while elevation, mental and physical, of the masses is going on far more rapidly than ever before – while the lowering of the death–rate proves that the average life is less trying, there swells louder and louder the cry that the evils are so great that nothing short of a social revolution can cure them. In presence of obvious improvements, joined with that increase of longevity which even alone yields conclusive proof of general amelioration, it is proclaimed, with increasing vehemence, that things are so bad that society must be pulled to pieces and re–organized on another plan. In this case, then, as in the previous cases instanced, in proportion as the evil decreases the denunciation of it increases; and as fast as natural causes are shown to be powerful there grows up the belief that they are powerless.

Not that the evils to be remedied are small. Let no one suppose that, by emphasizing the above paradox, I wish to make light of the sufferings which most men have to bear. The fates of the great majority have ever been, and doubtless still are, so sad that it is painful to think of them. Unquestionably the existing type of social organization is one which none who care for their kind can contemplate with satisfaction; and unquestionably men's activities accompanying this type are far from being admirable. The strong divisions of rank and the immense inequalities of means, are at variance with that ideal of human relations on which the sympathetic imagination likes to dwell; and the average conduct, under the pressure and excitement of social life as at present carried on, is in sundry respects repulsive. Though the many who revile competition strangely ignore the enormous benefits resulting from it – though they forget that most of all the appliances and products distinguishing civilization from savagery, and making possible the maintenance of a large population on a small area, have been developed by the struggle for existence – though they disregard the fact that while every man, as producer, suffers from the under-bidding of competitors, yet, as consumer, he is immensely advantaged by the cheapening of all he has to buy – though they persist in dwelling on the evils of competition and saying nothing of its benefits; yet it is not to be denied that the evils are great, and form a large set-off from the benefits. The system under which we at present live fosters dishonesty and lying. It prompts adulterations of countless kinds; it is answerable for the cheap imitations which eventually in many cases thrust the genuine articles out of the market; it leads to the use of short weights and false measures; it introduces bribery, which vitiates most trading relations, from those of the manufacturer and buyer down to those of the shopkeeper and servant; it encourages deception to such an extent that an assistant who cannot tell a falsehood with a good face is blamed; and often it gives the conscientious trader the choice between adopting the malpractices of his competitors, or greatly injuring his creditors by bankruptcy. Moreover, the extensive frauds, common throughout the commercial world and daily exposed in law-courts and newspapers, are largely due to the pressure under which competition places the higher industrial classes; and are otherwise due to that lavish expenditure which, as implying success in the commercial struggle, brings honour. With these minor evils must be joined the major one, that the distribution achieved by the system, gives to those who regulate and superintend, a share of the total produce which bears too large a ratio to the share it gives to the actual workers. Let it not be thought, then, that in saying what I have said above, I under-estimate those vices of our competitive system which, thirty years ago, I described and denounced.[1] But it is not a question of absolute evils; it is a

---

[1]   See essay on 'The Morals of Trade.' [*Westminster Review* (April, 1859), in *Essays: Scientific, Political and Speculative*, 3 vols, II (London: Williams

question of relative evils – whether the evils at present suffered are or are not less than the evils which would be suffered under another system – whether efforts for mitigation along the lines thus far followed are not more likely to succeed than efforts along utterly different lines.

This is the question here to be considered. I must be excused for first of all setting forth sundry truths which are, to some at any rate, tolerably familiar, before proceeding to draw inferences which are not so familiar.

Speaking broadly, every man works that he may avoid suffering. Here, remembrance of the pangs of hunger prompts him; and there, he is prompted by the sight of the slave-driver's lash. His immediate dread may be the punishment which physical circumstances will inflict, or may be punishment inflicted by human agency. He must have a master: but the master may be Nature or may be a fellow man. When he is under the impersonal coercion of Nature, we say that he is free; and when he is under the personal coercion of some one above him, we call him, according to the degree of his dependence, a slave, a serf, or a vassal. Of course I omit the small minority who inherit means: an incidental, and not a necessary, social element. I speak only of the vast majority, both cultured and uncultured, who maintain themselves by labour, bodily or mental, and must either exert themselves of their own unconstrained wills, prompted only by thoughts of naturally-resulting evils or benefits, or must exert themselves with constrained wills, prompted by thoughts of evils and benefits artificially resulting.

Men may work together in a society under either of these two forms of control: forms which, though in many cases mingled, are essentially contrasted. Using the word co-operation in its wide sense, and not in that restricted sense now commonly given to it, we may say that social life must be carried on by either voluntary co-operation or compulsory co-operation; or, to use Sir Henry Maine's words, the system must be that of *contract* or that of *status*[a] – that in which the individual is left

---

and Norgate, 1868), pp. 107–48.]

[a] Henry Sumner Maine (1822–88). In his *Ancient Law: its connection with the early history of society and its relation to modern ideas* (1861; London: John

to do the best he can by his spontaneous efforts and get success or failure according to his efficiency, and that in which he has his appointed place, works under coercive rule, and has his apportioned share of food, clothing and shelter.

The system of voluntary co-operation is that by which, in civilized societies, industry is now everywhere carried on. Under a simple form we have it on every farm, where the labourers, paid by the farmer himself and taking orders directly from him, are free to stay or go as they please. And of its more complex form an example is yielded by every manufacturing concern, in which, under partners, come clerks and managers, and under these, time-keepers and over-lookers, and under these, operatives of different grades. In each of these cases there is an obvious working together, or co-operation, of employer and employed, to obtain in one case a crop and in the other case a manufactured stock. And then, at the same time, there is a far more extensive, though unconscious, co-operation with other workers of all grades throughout the society. For while these particular employers and employed are severally occupied with their special kinds of work, other employers and employed are making other things needed for the carrying on of their lives as well as the lives of all others. This voluntary co-operation, from its simplest to its most complex forms, has the common trait that those concerned work together by consent. There is no one to force terms or to force acceptance. It is perfectly true that in many cases an employer may give, or an employé may accept, with reluctance: circumstances he says compel him. But what are the circumstances? In the one case there are goods ordered, or a contract entered into, which he cannot supply or execute without yielding; and in the other case he submits to a wage less than he likes because otherwise he will have no money wherewith to procure food and warmth. The general formula is not – 'Do this, or I will make you'; but it is – 'Do this, or leave your place and take the consequences.'

On the other hand compulsory co-operation is exemplified by an army – not so much by our own army, the service in which is under agreement for a specified period, but in a continental

Murray, 1905), Maine had written, '...we may say that the movement of the progressive societies has hitherto been a movement from *status to contract*', p. 170.

army, raised by conscription. Here, in time of peace the daily duties – cleaning, parade, drill, sentry work, and the rest – and in time of war the various actions of the camp and the battle-field, are done under command, without room for any exercise of choice. Up from the private soldier through the non-commissioned officers and the half-dozen or more grades of commissioned officers, the universal law is absolute obedience from the grade below to the grade above. The sphere of individual will is such only as is allowed by the will of the superior. Breaches of subordination are, according to their gravity, dealt with by deprivation of leave, extra drill, imprisonment, flogging, and in the last resort, shooting. Instead of the understanding that there must be obedience in respect of specified duties under pain of dismissal; the understanding now is – 'Obey in everything ordered under penalty of inflicted suffering and perhaps death.'

This form of co-operation, still exemplified in an army, has in days gone by been the form of co-operation throughout the civil population. Everywhere, and at all times, chronic war generates a militant type of structure, not in the body of soldiers only but throughout the community at large. Practically, while the conflict between societies is actively going on, and fighting is regarded as the only manly occupation, the society is the quiescent army and the army the mobilized society: the part which does not take part in battle, composed of slaves, serfs, women, &c., constituting the commissariat. Naturally, therefore, throughout the mass of inferior individuals constituting the commissariat, there is maintained a system of discipline identical in nature if less elaborate. The fighting body being, under such conditions, the ruling body, and the rest of the community being incapable of resistance, those who control the fighting body will, of course, impose their control upon the non-fighting body; and the *régime* of coercion will be applied to it with such modifications only as the different circumstances involve. Prisoners of war become slaves. Those who were free cultivators before the conquest of their country, become serfs attached to the soil. Petty chiefs become subject to superior chiefs; these smaller lords become vassals to over-lords; and so on up to the highest: the social ranks and powers being of like essential nature with the ranks and powers throughout the military organization. And while for the slaves compulsory co-operation is the unqualified system, a co-operation which is in part compulsory is the system that pervades all grades above. Each man's oath of fealty to his suzerain takes the form – 'I am your man.'

Throughout Europe, and especially in our own country, this system of compulsory co-operation gradually relaxed in rigour, while the system of voluntary co-operation step by step replaced it. As fast as war ceased to be the business of life, the social structure produced by war and appropriate to it, slowly became qualified by the social structure produced by industrial life and appropriate to it. In proportion as a decreasing part of the community was devoted to offensive and defensive activities, an increasing part became devoted to production and distribution. Growing more numerous, more powerful, and taking refuge in towns where it was less under the power of the militant class, this industrial population carried on its life under the system of voluntary co-operation. Though municipal governments and guild-regulations, partially pervaded by ideas and usages derived from the militant type of society, were in some degree coercive; yet production and distribution were in the main carried on under agreement – alike between buyers and sellers, and between masters and workmen. As fast as these social relations and forms of activity became dominant in urban populations, they influenced the whole community: compulsory co-operation lapsed more and more, through money commutation for services, military and civil; while divisions of rank became less rigid and class-power diminished. Until at length, restraints exercised by incorporated trades having fallen into desuetude, as well as the rule of rank over rank, voluntary co-operation became the universal principle. Purchase and sale became the law for all kinds of services as well as for all kinds of commodities.

The restlessness generated by pressure against the conditions of existence, perpetually prompts the desire to try a new position. Every one knows how long-continued rest in one attitude becomes wearisome – every one has found how even the best easy chair, at first rejoiced in, becomes after many hours intolerable; and the change to a hard seat, previously occupied and rejected, seems for a time to be a great relief. It is the same with incorporated humanity. Having by long struggles emancipated itself from the hard discipline of the ancient *régime*, and having discovered that the new *régime* into which it has grown, though relatively easy, is not without stresses and pains, its impatience with these prompts the wish to try another system; which other system is, in principle if not in appearance, the same as that which during past generations was escaped from with much rejoicing.

For as fast as the *régime* of contract is discarded the *régime* of status is of necessity adopted. As fast as voluntary co-operation is abandoned compulsory co-operation must be substituted. Some kind of organization labour must have; and if it is not that which arises by agreement under free competition, it must be that which is imposed by authority. Unlike in appearance and names as it may be to the old order of slaves and serfs, working under masters, who were coerced by barons, who were themselves vassals of dukes or kings, the new order wished for, constituted by workers under foremen of small groups, overlooked by superintendents, who are subject to higher local managers, who are controlled by superiors of districts, themselves under a central government, must be essentially the same in principle. In the one case, as in the other, there must be established grades, and enforced subordination of each grade to the grades above. This is a truth which the communist or the socialist does not dwell upon. Angry with the existing system under which each of us takes care of himself, while all of us see that each has fair play, he thinks how much better it would be for all of us to take care of each of us; and he refrains from thinking of the machinery by which this is to be done. Inevitably, if each is to be cared for by all, then the embodied all must get the means – the necessaries of life. What it gives to each must be taken from the accumulated contributions; and it must, therefore, require from each his proportion – must tell him how much he has to give to the general stock in the shape of production, that he may have so much in the shape of sustentation. Hence, before he can be provided for, he must put himself under orders, and obey those who say what he shall do, and at what hours, and where; and who give him his share of food, clothing, and shelter. If competition is excluded, and with it buying and selling, there can be no voluntary exchange of so much labour for so much produce; but there must be apportionment of the one to the other by appointed officers. This apportionment must be enforced. Without alternative the work must be done, and without alternative the benefit, whatever it may be, must be accepted. For the worker may not leave his place at will and offer himself elsewhere. Under such a system he cannot be accepted elsewhere, save by order of the authorities. And it is manifest that a standing order would forbid employment in one place of an insubordinate member from another place: the system could not be worked if the workers were severally allowed to go or come as they pleased. With corporals and sergeants under them, the captains of industry must carry out the orders of their colonels, and these [*sic.*] of their generals, up to the council of the commander–in–chief; and obedience must be required throughout the industrial army as throughout a fighting army. 'Do your prescribed duties, and take your apportioned rations', must be the rule of the one as of the other.

'Well, be it so;' replies the socialist. 'The workers will appoint their own officers, and these will always be subject to criticisms of the mass they regulate. Being thus in fear of public opinion, they will be sure to act judiciously and fairly; or when they do not, will be deposed by the popular vote, local or general. Where will be the grievance of being under superiors, when the superiors themselves are under democratic control?' And in this attractive vision the socialist has full belief.

Iron and brass are simpler things than flesh and blood, and dead wood than living nerve; and a machine constructed of the one works in more definite ways than an organism constructed of the other,– especially when the machine is worked by the inorganic forces of steam or water, while the organism is worked by the forces of living nerve-centres. Manifestly, then, the ways in which the machine will work are much more readily calculable than the ways in which the organism will work. Yet in how few cases does the inventor foresee rightly the actions of his new apparatus! Read the patent-list, and it will be found that not more than one device in fifty turns out to be of any service. Plausible as his scheme seemed to the inventor, one or other hitch prevents the intended operation, and brings out a widely different result from that which he wished.

What, then, shall we say of these [*sic.*] schemes which have to do not with dead matters and forces, but with complex living organisms working in ways less readily foreseen, and which involve the co-operation of multitudes of such organisms? Even the units out of which this re-arranged body politic is to be formed are often incomprehensible. Every one is from time to time surprised by others' behaviour, and even by the deeds of relatives who are best known to him. Seeing, then, how uncertainly any one can foresee the actions of an individual, how can he with any certainty foresee the operation of a social structure? He proceeds on the assumption that all concerned will judge rightly and act fairly – will think as they ought to think, and act as they ought to act; and he assumes this regardless of the daily experiences which show him that men do neither the one nor the other, and forgetting that the complaints he makes against the existing system show his belief to be that men have neither the wisdom nor the rectitude which his plan requires them to have.

Paper constitutions raise smiles on the faces of those who have observed their results; and paper social systems similarly affect those who have contemplated the available evidence. How little the men who wrought the French revolution and were chiefly concerned in setting up the new governmental apparatus, dreamt that one of the early actions of this apparatus would be to behead them all! How little the men who drew up the American Declaration of Independence and framed the Republic, anticipated that after some generations the legislature would lapse into the hands of wire-pullers; that its doings would turn upon the contests of office-seekers, that political action would be everywhere vitiated by the intrusion of a foreign element holding the balance between parties; that electors, instead of judging for themselves, would habitually be led to the polls in thousands by their 'bosses'; and that respectable men would be driven out of public life by the insults and slanders of professional politicians. Nor were there better previsions in those who gave constitutions to the various other states of the New World in which unnumbered revolutions have shown with wonderful persistence the contrast between the expected results of political systems and the achieved results. It has been no less thus with proposed systems of social re-organization, so far as they have been tried. Save where celibacy has been insisted on, their history has been everywhere one of disaster; ending with the history of Cabet's[b] Icarian colony lately given by one of its members, Madame Fleury Robinson, in *The Open Court* – a history of splittings, re-splittings, re-re-splittings, accompanied by numerous individual secessions and final dissolution. And for the failure of such social schemes, as for the failure of the political schemes, there has been one general cause.

Metamorphosis is the universal law, exemplified throughout the Heavens and on the Earth: especially throughout the organic world; and above all in the animal division of it. No creature, save the simplest and the most minute, commences its existence in a form like that which it eventually assumes; and in most cases the unlikeness is great – so great that kinship between the first and the last forms would be incredible were it not daily demonstrated in every poultry-yard and every garden. More than this is true. The changes of form are often several: each of them being an apparently complete transformation – egg, larva, pupa, imago, for example. And this universal metamorphosis, displayed alike in the development of a planet and of every seed which germinates on its surface, holds also of societies, whether taken as wholes or in their separate institutions. No one of them ends as it begins; and the difference between its original structure and its ultimate structure is such that, at the outset, change of the one into the other would have seemed incredible. In the rudest tribe the chief, obeyed as leader in war, loses his distinctive position when the fighting is over; and even where continued warfare has produced permanent chieftainship, the chief, building his own hut, getting his own

---

[b] Etienne Cabet (1788–1856), French socialist who attempted to follow the example of Robert Owen in putting into practice his utopian socialist ideas. In 1848, he sent an expedition of 1,500 settlers to a tract of land in Texas. Community of property was to be their guiding principle. However, the settlers soon became disenchanted.

food, making his own implements, differs from others only by his predominant influence. There is no sign that in course of time, by conquests and unions of tribes, and consolidations of clusters so formed with other such clusters, until a nation has been produced, there will originate from the primitive chief, one who, as czar or emperor, surrounded with pomp and ceremony, has despotic power over scores of millions, exercised through hundreds of thousands of soldiers and hundreds of thousands of officials. When the early Christian missionaries, having humble externals and passing self-denying lives, spread over pagan Europe, preaching forgiveness of injuries and the returning of good for evil, no one dreamt that in course of time their representatives would form a vast hierarchy, possessing everywhere a large part of the land, distinguished by the haughtiness of its members grade above grade, ruled by military bishops who led their retainers to battle, and headed by a pope exercising supreme power over kings. So, too, has it been with that very industrial system which many are now so eager to replace. In its original form there was no prophecy of the factory system or kindred organizations of workers. Differing from them only as being the head of his house, the master worked along with his apprentices and a journeyman or two, sharing with them his table and accommodation, and himself selling their joint produce. Only with industrial growth did there come employment of a larger number of assistants and a relinquishment, on the part of the master, of all other business than that of superintendence. And only in the course of recent times did there evolve the organizations under which the labours of hundreds and thousands of men receiving wages are regulated by various orders of paid officials under a single or multiple head. These originally small, semi-socialistic, groups of producers, like the compound families or house-communities of early ages, slowly dissolved because they could not hold their ground: the larger establishments, with better subdivision of labour, succeeded because they ministered to the wants of society more effectually. But we need not go back through the centuries to trace transformations sufficiently great and unexpected. On the day when £30,000 a year in aid of education was voted as an experiment, the name of idiot would have been given to an opponent who prophesied that in fifty years the sum spent through imperial taxes and local rates would amount to £10,000,000, or who said that the aid to education would be followed by aids to feeding and clothing, or who said that parents and children, alike deprived of all option, would, even if starving, be compelled by fine or imprisonment to conform, and receive that which, with papal assumption, the State calls education. No one, I say, would have dreamt that out of so innocent-looking a germ would have so quickly evolved this tyrannical system, tamely submitted to by people who fancy themselves free.

Thus in social arrangements, as in all other things, change is inevitable. It is foolish to suppose that new institutions set up, will long retain the character given them by those who set them up. Rapidly or slowly they will be transformed into institutions unlike those intended – so unlike as even to be unrecognizable by their devisers. And what, in the case before us, will be the metamorphosis? The answer pointed to by instances above given, and warranted by various analogies, is manifest.

A cardinal trait in all advancing organization is the development of the regulative apparatus. If the parts of a whole are to act together, there must be appliances by which their actions are directed; and in proportion as the whole is large and complex, and has many requirements to be met by many agencies, the directive apparatus must be extensive, elaborate, and powerful. That it is thus with individual organisms needs no saying; and that it must be thus with social organisms is obvious. Beyond the regulative apparatus such as in our own society is required for carrying on national defence and maintaining public order and personal safety, there must, under the *régime* of socialism, be a regulative apparatus everywhere controlling all kinds of production and distribution, and everywhere apportioning the shares of products of each kind required for each locality, each working establishment, each individual. Under our existing voluntary co-operation, with its free contracts and its competition, production and distribution need no official oversight. Demand and supply, and the desire of each man to gain a living by supplying the needs of his fellows, spontaneously evolve that wonderful system whereby a great city has its food daily brought round to all doors or stored at adjacent shops; has clothing for its citizens everywhere at hand in multitudinous varieties; has its houses and furniture and fuel ready made or stocked in each locality; and has mental pabulum from halfpenny papers, hourly hawked round, to weekly shoals of novels, and less abundant books of instruction, furnished without stint for small payments. And throughout the kingdom, production as well as distribution is similarly carried on with the smallest amount of superintendence which proves efficient; while the quantities of the numerous commodities required daily in each locality are adjusted without any other agency than the pursuit of profit. Suppose now that this industrial *régime* of willinghood, acting spontaneously, is replaced by a *régime* of industrial obedience, enforced by public officials. Imagine the vast administration required for that distribution of all commodities to all people in every city, town and village, which is now effected by traders! Imagine, again, the still more vast administration required for doing all that farmers, manufacturers, and merchants do; having not only its various orders of local superintendents, but its sub–centres and chief centres needed for apportioning the quantities of each thing everywhere needed, and the adjustment of them to the requisite times. Then add the staffs wanted for working mines, railways, roads, canals; the staffs required for conducting the importing and exporting businesses and the administration of mercantile shipping; the staffs required for supplying towns not only with water and gas but with locomotion by tramways, omnibuses, and other vehicles, and for the distribution of power, electric and other. Join with these the existing postal, telegraphic, and telephonic administrations; and finally those of the police and army, by which the dictates of this immense consolidated regulative system are to be everywhere enforced. Imagine all this, and then ask what will be the position of the actual workers! Already on the continent, where governmental organizations are more elaborate and coercive than here, there are chronic complaints of the tyranny of bureaucracies – the *hauteur* and brutality of their members. What will these become when not only the more public actions of citizens are controlled, but there is added this far more extensive control of all their respective daily duties? What will happen when the various divisions of this vast army of officials, united by interests common to officialism – the interests of the regulators *versus* those of the regulated – have at their command whatever force is needful to suppress insubordination and act as 'saviours of society'? Where will be the actual diggers and miners and smelters and weavers, when those who order and superintend, everywhere arranged class above class, have come, after some generations, to intermarry with those of kindred grades, under feelings such as are operative in existing classes; and when there have been so produced a series of castes rising in superiority; and when all these, having everything in their own power, have arranged modes of living for their own advantage: eventually forming a new aristocracy far more elaborate and better organized than the old? How will the individual worker fare if he is dissatisfied with his treatment – thinks that he has not an adequate share of the products, or has more to do than can rightly be demanded, or wishes to undertake a function for which he feels himself fitted but which is not thought proper for him by his superiors, or desires to make an independent career for himself? This dissatisfied unit in the immense machine will be told he must submit or go. The mildest penalty for disobedience will be industrial excommunication. And if an international organization of labour is formed as proposed, exclusion in one country will mean exclusion in all others – industrial excommunication will mean starvation.

That things must take this course is a conclusion reached not by deduction only, nor only by induction from those experiences of the past instanced above, nor only from consideration of the analogies furnished by organisms of all orders; but it is reached also by observation of cases daily under our eyes. The truth that the regulative structure always tends to increase in power, is illustrated by every established body of men. The history of each learned society, or society for other purpose, shows how the staff, permanent or partially permanent sways the proceedings and determines the actions of the society with but little resistance, even when most members of the society disapprove: the repugnance to anything like a revolutionary step being ordinarily an efficient deterrent. So is it with joint-stock companies – those owning railways for example. The plans of a board of directors are usually authorized with little or no discussion; and if there is any considerable opposition, this is forthwith crushed by an overwhelming number of proxies sent by those who always support the existing administration. Only when the misconduct is extreme does the resistance of shareholders suffice to displace the ruling body. Nor is it otherwise with societies formed of working men and having the interests of labour especially at heart – the Trades Unions. In these, too, the regulative agency becomes all powerful. Their members, even when they dissent from the policy pursued, habitually yield to the authorities they have set up. As they cannot secede without making enemies of their fellow workmen, and often losing all chance of employment, they succumb. We are shown, too, by the late congress, that already, in the general organization of Trades Unions so recently formed, there are complaints of 'wire-pullers' and 'bosses' and 'permanent officials.'[c] If, then, this supremacy of the regulators is seen in bodies of quite modern origin, formed of men who have, in many of the cases instanced, unhindered powers of asserting their independence, what will the supremacy of the regulators become in long-established bodies, in bodies which have grown vast and highly organized, and in bodies which, instead of controlling only a small part of the unit's life, control the whole of his life?

Again there will come the rejoinder – 'We shall guard against all that. Everybody will be educated; and all, with their eyes constantly open to the abuse of power, will be quick to prevent it.' The worth of these expectations would be small even could we not identify the causes which will bring disappointment; for in human affairs the most promising schemes go wrong in ways which no one anticipated. But in this case the going wrong will be necessitated by causes which are conspicuous. The working

---

[c] At the Trades Union Congress at Liverpool in 1890, which was dominated by the issue of the Eight Hours Day, leaders of the new unions attacked the 'slow-going officialism' of delegates from older unions such as the cotton operatives in Lancashire. (They had objected to the Eight Hours Day on the grounds that this would give an advantage to their competitors.) The general feeling among new union leaders was that 'energetic men and...men of capacity will influence the rank and file of the unions in spite of the wire-pulling of those who seek to oppose them.' *The Times* (12 September 1890), p. 6.

of institutions is determined by men's characters; and the existing defects in their characters will inevitably bring about the results above indicated. There is no adequate endowment of those sentiments required to prevent the growth of a despotic bureaucracy.

Were it needful to dwell on indirect evidence, much might be made of that furnished by the behaviour of the so-called Liberal party – a party which, relinquishing the original conception of a leader as a mouthpiece for a known and accepted policy, thinks itself bound to accept a policy which its leader springs upon it without consent or warning – a party so utterly without the feeling and idea implied by liberalism, as not to resent this trampling on the right of private judgement which constitutes the root of liberalism – nay, a party which vilifies as renegade liberals, those of its members who refuse to surrender their independence! But without occupying space with indirect proofs that the mass of men have not the natures required to check the development of tyrannical officialism, it will suffice to contemplate the direct proofs furnished by those classes among whom the socialistic idea most predominates, and who think themselves most interested in propagating it – the operative classes. These would constitute the great body of the socialistic organization, and their characters would determine its nature. What, then, are their characters as displayed in such organizations as they have already formed?

Instead of the selfishness of the employing classes and the selfishness of competition, we are to have the unselfishness of a mutually-aiding system. How far is this unselfishness now shown in the behaviour of working men to one another? What shall we say to the rules limiting the numbers of new hands admitted into each trade, or to the rules which hinder ascent from inferior classes of workers to superior classes? One does not see in such regulations any of that altruism by which socialism is to be pervaded. Contrariwise, one sees a pursuit of private interests no less keen than among traders. Hence, unless we suppose that men's natures will be suddenly exalted, we must conclude that the pursuit of private interests will sway the doings of all the component classes in a socialistic society.

With passive disregard of others' claims goes active encroachment on them. 'Be one of us or we will cut off your means of living', is the usual threat of each Trades Union to outsiders of the same trade. While their members insist on their own freedom to combine and fix the rates at which they will work (as they are perfectly justified in doing), the freedom of those who disagree with them is not only denied but the assertion of it is treated as a crime. Individuals who maintain their rights to make their own contracts are vilified as 'blacklegs' and 'traitors,' and meet with violence which would be merciless were there no legal penalties and no police. Along with this trampling on the liberties of men of their own class, there goes peremptory dictation of the employing class: not prescribed terms and working arrangements only shall be conformed to, but none save those belonging to their body shall be employed – nay, in some case, there shall be a strike if the employer carries on transactions with trading bodies that give work to non-union men. Here, then, we are variously shown by Trades Unions, or at any rate by the newer Trades Unions, a determination to impose their regulations without regard to the rights of those who are to be coerced. So complete is the inversion of ideas and sentiments that maintenance of these rights is regarded as vicious and trespass upon them as virtuous.[2]

Along with this aggressiveness in one direction there goes submissiveness in another direction. The coercion of outsiders by unionists is paralleled only by their subjection to their leaders. That they may conquer in the struggle they surrender their individual liberties and individual judgments, and show no

---

[2] Marvellous are the conclusions men reach when once they desert the simple principle, that each man should be allowed to pursue the objects of life, restrained only by the limits which the similar pursuits of their objects by other men impose. A generation ago we heard loud assertions of 'the right to labour', that is, the right to have labour provided; and there are still not a few who think the community bound to find work for each person. Compare this with the doctrine current in France at the time when the monarchical power culminated; namely, that 'the right of working is a royal right which the prince can sell and the subjects must buy.' This contrast is startling enough; but a contrast still more startling is being provided for us. We now see a resuscitation of the despotic doctrine, differing only by the substitution of Trades Unions for kings. For now that Trades Unions are becoming universal, and each artisan has to pay prescribed moneys to one or another of them, with the alternative of being a non-unionist to whom work is denied by force, it has come to this, that the right to labour is a Trade Union right, which the Trade Union can sell and the individual worker must buy!

resentment however dictatorial may be the rule exercised over them. Everywhere we see such subordination that bodies of workmen unanimously leave their work or return to it as their authorities order them. Nor do they resist when taxed all round to support strikers whose acts they may or may not approve, but instead, ill-treat recalcitrant members of their body who do not subscribe.

The traits thus shown must be operative in any new social organization, and the question to be asked is – What will result from their operation when they are relieved from all restraints? At present the separate bodies of men displaying them are in the midst of a society partially passive, partially antagonistic; are subject to the criticisms and reprobations of an independent press; and are under the control of law, enforced by police. If in these circumstances these bodies habitually take courses which override individual freedom, what will happen when, instead of being only scattered parts of the community, governed by their separate sets of regulators, they constitute the whole community, governed by a consolidated system of such regulators; when functionaries of all orders, including those who officer the press, form parts of the regulative organization; and when the law is both enacted and administered by this regulative organization? The fanatical adherents of a social theory are capable of taking any measures, no matter how extreme, for carrying out their views: holding, like the merciless priesthoods of past times, that the end justifies the means. And when a general socialistic organization has been established, the vast, ramified, and consolidated body of those who direct its activities, using without check whatever coercion seems to them needful in the interests of the system (which will practically become their own interests) will have no hesitation in imposing their rigorous rule over the entire lives of the actual workers; until, eventually, there is developed an official oligarchy, with its various grades, exercising a tyranny more gigantic and more terrible than any which the world has seen.

Let me again repudiate an erroneous inference. Any one who supposes that the foregoing argument implies contentment with things as they are, makes a profound mistake. The present social state is transitional, as past social states have been transitional. There will, I hope and believe, come a future social state differing as much from the present as the present differs from the past with its mailed barons and defenceless serfs. In *Social Statics*,[d] as well as in *The Study of Sociology*[e] and in *Political Institutions*,[f] is clearly shown the desire for an organization more conducive to the happiness of men at large than that which exists. My opposition to socialism results from the belief that it would stop the progress to such a higher state and bring back a lower state. Nothing but the slow modification of human nature by the discipline of social life can produce permanently advantageous changes.

A fundamental error pervading the thinking of nearly all parties, political and social, is that evils admit of immediate and radical remedies. 'If you will but do this, the mischief will be prevented.' 'Adopt my plan and the suffering will disappear.' 'The corruption will unquestionably be cured by enforcing this measure.' Everywhere one meets with beliefs, expressed or implied, of these kinds. They are all ill-founded. It is possible to remove causes which intensify the evils; it is possible to change the evils from one form into another; and it is possible, and very common, to exacerbate the evils by the efforts made to prevent them; but anything like immediate cure is impossible. In the course of thousands of years mankind have, by multiplication, been forced out of that original savage state in which small numbers supported themselves on wild food, into the civilized state in which the food required for supporting great numbers can be got only by continuous labour. The nature required for this last mode of life is widely different from the nature required for the first; and long-continued pains have to be passed through in remoulding the one into the other. Misery has necessarily to be borne by a constitution out of harmony with its conditions; and a constitution inherited from primitive men is out of harmony with the conditions imposed on existing men. Hence it is impossible to establish forthwith a satisfactory social state. No such nature as that which has filled

---

[d] *Social Statics: or the conditions essential to human happiness specified, and the first of them developed* (London: Watts & Co., 1851).

[e] *The Study of Sociology* (London: H.S. King, 1873).

[f] *Political Institutions* (1882), vol. II, part V of *The Principles of Sociology*, 3 vols (London: Williams & Norgate, 1876–96).

Europe with millions of armed men, here eager for conquest and there for revenge – no such nature as that which prompts the nations called Christians to vie with one another in filibustering expeditions all over the world, regardless of the claims of aborigines, while their tens of thousands of priests of the religion of love look on approvingly – no such nature as that which, in dealing with weaker races, goes beyond the primitive rule of life for life, and for one life takes many lives – no such nature, I say, can, by any device, be framed into a harmonious community. The root of all well–ordered social action is a sentiment of justice, which at once insists on personal freedom and is solicitous for the like freedom of others; and there at present exists but a very inadequate amount of this sentiment.

Hence the need for further long continuance of a social discipline which requires each man to carry on his activities with due regard to the like claims of others to carry on their activities; and which, while it insists that he shall have all the benefits his conduct naturally brings, insists also that he shall not saddle on others the evils his conduct naturally brings: unless they freely undertake to bear them. And hence the belief that endeavours to elude this discipline will not only fail, but will bring worse evils than those to be escaped.

It is not, then, chiefly in the interests of the employing classes that socialism is to be resisted, but much more in the interests of the employed classes. In one way or other production must be regulated; and the regulators, in the nature of things, must always be a small class as compared with the actual producers. Under voluntary co–operation as at present carried on, the regulators, pursing their personal interests, take as large a share of the produce as they can get; but, as we are daily shown by Trades Union successes, are restrained in the selfish pursuit of their ends. Under that compulsory co–operation which socialism would necessitate, the regulators, pursuing their personal interests with no less selfishness, could not be met by the combined resistance of free workers; and their power, unchecked as now by refusals to work save on prescribed terms, would grow and ramify and consolidate till it became irresistible, The ultimate result, as I have before pointed out, must be a society like that of ancient Peru, dreadful to contemplate, in which the mass of the people, elaborately regimented in groups of 10, 50, 100, 500, and 1000, ruled by officers of corresponding grades, and tied to their districts, were superintended in their private lives as well as in their industries, and toiled hopelessly for the support of the governmental organization.

INDEX

absolute authority 75
absolute government 87
absolute monarchy 76, 94, 95
absolute power 76
absolute state 86
absolutism 15, 72, 78–79, 86–88, 93
absolutism, dynastic 71
Afghanistan 63
Afrancesados 79
agricultural land, sale of 125
Agricultural Holdings Act (1875) 112
agriculture 127
Albert, Charles 82
America 50, 73, 107–108, 129, 135
American Declaration of Independence 145
American revolution 17
American Union 103
Amsterdam 73
anarchism 32
ancient *régime* 143
Aquinas, St. Thomas 28
Arcadian region 66
aristocracy 8, 54, 69, 70, 76, 94, 150
aristocratic rule 135
Aristotelian 100
army 140
army commissions, purchase of 7
army, flogging in 58
Arnold, Matthew 25, 27
artisans 102–103, 107, 109

Assaye 63
Athens 73
Austin, John 9
Austria 80, 82, 89, 91–94
Austria, Italian provinces of 82
Austrian empire 95
Austrian power, restoration in Italy 84
Austro-Hungarian empire 16
authority 68, 73, 86, 107, 143
authority, spiritual 14

Babœuf, François Noël 69
Bach, Alexander von 80
Baden 92
barbarism 16, 94
Barnburners 47
Beaconsfield, Lord 112
Belgian revolution 81
Berlin 83
Berne 73
Bonaparte, Napoleon 77–78, 80–82
Bonapartism 78
Bonapartists 81
Brabant rising 67
Bright, John 7–8, 21–22, 25–26, 97, 103
Britain, seventeenth-century 35–36
British empire 10, 17, 64, 95
British State 17, 38
Bryce, James 17, 36
bureaucracies, tyranny of 149
bureaucracy, despotic 152
Burke, Edmund 15, 18, 25, 38,

72, 90–91
Byron, Lord 47

Cabet, Etienne 146
Cairns, Sir later Lord Hugh
    McCalmont 20, 97–98, 100,
    104, 106, 109–110, 125
Calvinism 8
Campanella, Tommaso 66
capitalists 102
Carbonari 81, 83
cathedral chapters, reform of 114
Catholic countries 74
Catholic hierarchy 17
Catholicism 14–15, 67
Cawnpore 63
Cæsar 75
Cæsarean system 75
centralisation 15, 86, 93–95, 121
Charity Commissioners Act
    (1853) 114
Charlemagne 88
Charles, king 90
Chartists 29
chieftainship 146
Christendom 88
Christian 25, 75
Christian missionaries 147
Christian philosophers 28
Christian powers 71
Christianity 25, 61, 88–89
church rates 7
Church 76, 88–89, 101, 147
Church, administration of 114
Church, authority of 67
Church, Catholic 14–17
Church, Eastern 81
Church, independence of 86
Church property 70
Church=Holy Roman Empire 88

citizens 117
citizenship 25
City of the Sun 66
civil privileges 118
civil society 69, 75, 95
civilisation 16, 87–88, 92, 138
civilised man 90
civilised world 68
class, 'regulated' 34
class 7, 37, 49, 75, 86, 97, 107–
    109, 119, 150, 153, 156
class interests 109, 113
class, landowners 110
class privilege 113
class representation 97–100, 103,
    106, 108, 110
class representatives 107
class rights, theory of 108
class, small proprietors 125
classes 20, 69, 74, 97–98, 100,
    102, 106, 108, 152
classes, balance of 104
classes, commercial 104
classes, Dissenting 10
classes, educated 23
classes, employed 156
classes, employing 152, 153, 156
classes, landed 30, 104
classes, lower 8, 137
classes, middle 7, 23, 29–30, 69,
    102, 105, 109, 136
classes, operative 152
classes, upper 136–37
classes, working 7, 11, 20, 23–
    24, 30, 98, 101–102, 104,
    106–107
clergy, liberty of 59–60
Clovis 76
Cobden, Richard 7
Coke, Sir Edward 22

Coleridge, Samuel Taylor 25
collectivism 19, 22–23
common good 25, 27, 38, 119
Common Law, English 19, 22,
    24, 37
communism 69
competition 138, 144, 148, 152
Complete Suffrage Union 29
compulsion 118
Concordat 89
Conservatism 9, 109
Conspiracy and Protection of
    Property Act 21
constitutionalism 95
constitutions, paper 145
contract 111–112, 129–30,
    139
contract, *régime* of 32
Convention 90
Convocation, leaders of 107
co-operation 139–42
co-operation, compulsory 139–
    43, 156
co-operation, voluntary 33, 139–
    40, 142–43, 148, 156
corn, protection of 102
Corn Laws, Repeal of (1846) 7,
    35, 114
crusades 56

Dalberg-Acton, John Emerich
    Edward, First Baron Acton
    5, 14–18, 37, 40, 66–96
Dante 83
Danube, steam navigation of 38
de Toqueville, Alexis de 64
democracy 7–9, 15, 19, 23–24,
    26, 31–32, 50, 73, 76, 85,
    87, 95–96, 134
democratic equality 95

democratic Reformers 97
democrats 99
Derby 29
Derby, Lord 125
despotism 75, 86–87
Dicey, Albert Venn 5, 19–24,
    34, 37, 40, 97–110
Dickens, Charles 11, 57
disenfranchisement 99
Disraeli, Benjamin 7, 11, 57, 104
Dissent 7
Dissenters 8
Dissenting beliefs 29
diversity 87
divine right of kings 31
Dnieper, suspension bridge over
    38
drunkenness 131–33, 136
Dutch 82
dwellings, unwholesome 120

Ecclesiastical Duties and
    Revenues Act (1940)
    114
educated opinions 58–59
education 7–8, 59, 99, 120, 122,
    124, 136, 147–48
education, compulsory 27, 34,
    120
Education Act (1868) 116
Education Act (1870) 116
Education Acts 112, 133
emigration 129
Employers Liability Act (1880)
    26, 111
employment 28, 115–26, 144
enfranchisement of the masses 99
England 7–9, 14, 17, 23, 38, 49,
    53, 56, 64, 70–71, 77, 79,
    125, 128, 134–35

English Civil War 38
English Constitution 97
English farmer(s) 112, 127–29
English individualism 37
English legislation 116
English Liberalism, late-
    Victorian 39
English liberty 38, 72
English political institutions 37
English society 10–11, 19–20,
    108
English tradition 36, 39
English view of nationality 85
English virtues 38
Englishmen 53, 56, 91, 109
Englishness 36–39
equality 69, 75–77, 94
Europe 71, 72, 80, 81, 142, 147,
    156
European system 69, 71
eviction 130
evolution, theory of 30

Factory Acts 112, 115, 133
Factory Acts Extension and
    Workshops Regulation Act
    (1867) 115
federalism 15, 73
Fénelon, François de Salignac de
    La Mothe 70
feudalism 76
First Reform Act 113, 115
First World War, post 36
First World War 39
Flanders 91
Florence 92
Forty-five Rebellion 71
France 15, 21, 50, 73–74, 76–77,
    79, 84, 91
franchise 7–9, 19–20, 110, 135

franchise, extension of (1867) 19,
    109
franchise, extension of 7, 99
free competition 143
free contracts 148
freedom 26–28, 32, 38, 75, 78–
    79, 82, 85, 87, 89, 93–94,
    96, 113–14, 117–22, 126,
    130–32, 133, 153
freedom, era of 32
freedom, individual 113
freedom, law of equal 30, 38
freedom, moral 28
freedom of contract 27–28, 111–
    34
freedom, personal 25, 32, 56
freedom, public 124
Freeman, Edward Augustus 17
French 17, 38, 82, 92
French administration 77, 82
French Assembly 101
French authority 82
French Bourbons 71
French history 76
French institutions 79
French monarchy 72
French people 73
French power, fall of 79
French revolution (1848) 82, 84,
    101
French Revolution 46, 56, 67–68,
    72, 74, 76, 145
French state 73
French supremacy 79
French view of nationality 85

Gardiner, Samuel Rawson 36
Gaskell, Mrs Elizabeth 11, 57
Gatton 105
Gaul 75

Genoa 80
'gentleman' 49–50
gentlemen, country 107
George III 103
Germans 38, 71
Germany 71, 77, 83, 91
Giovane Europa 84
Giovane Italia 83–84
Gironde 46
Gladstone, William Ewart 7, 17, 26, 97, 114
Gladstone, Mary 18
Glorious Revolution 8
Görres, Johann Joseph von 78
government 22, 51–54, 63, 65, 70, 73, 74, 83, 87, 105, 121, 130
government, central 116, 121, 143
government expenditure 7
government, free 103
government, legacy of aristocratic 39
government, 'militant' aristocratic 39
governmental organizations 149
Great Rebellion 67
Greece 73
Greek revolution 81
Green, Thomas Hill 5, 24–29, 38, 111–134
Ground Game Act (1880) 26, 111, 126
guild-regulations 142

Hale, Sir Matthew 22
Hapsburgs 71
Harcourt, Sir William Vernon 121

Hayek, Friedrich August von 39
health 115, 117, 120, 123
hereditary aristocracy 7
hereditary claims 89
hereditary crown 70
hereditary nobility 76
historical continuity 18
history, political influence of 74
Hohenzollern dynasty 71
Holland, republic of 70
Holy Alliance 79
Holy Alliance, governments of 80
Home Secretary 121
House of Commons 18, 97, 114–16
House of Lords 18, 22
house-communities 147
£10 householders 98, 108–109
housing 28, 123
Howard family 52
Humboldt, Wilhelm von 78
Hunkers 47
Hus, Jan 67
Hutton, Richard Holt 13, 14

Icarian colony 146
Idealism 25
imperial consciousness 10
imperialism 74
incorporated trades 142
Independents 38
India 10–11, 63–64
India, government of 63
India, Viceroy's Council in 10
Indian empire 63
Indies 71
individualism 19–24
industrial excommunication 150
industrial life 142
industrial obedience, *régime* of

149
industrialism 30, 32–33, 38
industry, free 119
inequality 77
intellectual cultivation 66
Ireland 15, 17, 107, 128
Ireland, emancipation of 89
Ireland, peasant farmers 128
Irish Church 7–8
Irish farmers 129
Irish Home Rule Bills 24
Irish Home Rule 15, 17, 36
Italy 71, 77, 79, 81–84, 91

Jacobites 71
joint-stock companies 34, 150
Joseph, Francis 84
justice, sentiment of 156

Kingsley, Charles 11, 57
Know-nothings 47

labour 102, 115–17, 119–20,
    123–24, 143, 147, 151, 153,
    155
labour, international organization
    of 150
Labour of Children and Young
    Persons in Mills and
    Factories Act (1833) 115
labourer(s) 102, 123–24, 129,
    136, 140
land 21, 27, 11, 121–24
land, distribution of 126
land, English 126
land, improvement of 126
land nationalization 30
Land Law 124
Land Laws, reform of 112
Land League 129

landed aristocracy 22
landlord(s) 26, 111–13, 125–29
land-owner/landowners 27, 102,
    125
Latin Europe 76
Latin nations 77
law, code of 76
law, compulsion of 122
law, moral 13
law, public 71
law, rule of 23
law, sanction of 111
law, system of 115
law(s) 19, 22, 26, 68, 74, 88, 90,
    101–102, 111, 117, 120–24,
    127–28, 131–34, 146, 154
laws, factory 116, 124
laws, public health 112
laws, revocation of 85
laws, school 116, 124
league of nations, international 84
learned societies 34
leases 127–28
legal profession 22
legislation 123, 126, 134
legislative conservatism 23
legitimacy 71, 82, 85
Leicester 26
Leicester, Lord 125
liberal 5, 7, 9–10, 17, 18, 19,
    20, 25, 36, 47, 49–50, 54–
    55, 77
liberal England 40
liberal imperial spirit 60
liberal movement 81, 83
liberal radicalism 29, 31, 35
Liberal 47–48, 98, 111–112
Liberal Association 26
Liberal Catholic 14
Liberal Legislation 111–34

Liberal Licensing Act (1872) 130
Liberal party 10, 112, 152
liberalism 5, 7–11, 13–15, 17,
    18, 19, 24–28, 33, 35, 36,
    37, 46–65, 81, 83, 152
liberalism, British 35
liberalism, Dissenting 7, 27
liberalism, French 72
liberalism, ideal of modern 87
liberalism, individualist 19, 24
liberalism, mid-Victorian 25, 36
liberalism, political 60
liberalism, radical 9, 17, 28
liberalism, spurious 49
liberalism, traditional 24, 28
liberalism, true 63–64
Liberalism, 'Manchester' 11
Liberalism, Dissenting 8
Liberalism, Radical 7
liberals 13, 34, 36, 37, 60, 62,
    64–65, 70, 79
liberals, radical 35
liberals, true 64
Liberals 98, 113, 126
Liberals, philosophic 97
liberty 9, 14, 22, 25, 32, 34, 37,
    38, 77, 81, 86–87, 92–93,
    95–96, 103, 114, 125, 131–
    33
liberty, individual 13, 113, 117
liberty, national 13, 15, 85, 89
liberty, personal 22
liberty, political 78
liberty, religious 89
licensing law 132
Licensing Laws 113
'Lincolnshire custom' 127
liquor law 133
Liquor Law 124
literature 59, 83, 88, 136

living conditions,
    improvement of 136
local authorities 73, 94, 121
Local Government Act (1888)
    114
Locke, John 28
London 19, 121
Lorimer, Professor James 105–
    106
Luther, Martin 67

Macaulay, Thomas Babington,
    First Baron 9, 16
Mackintosh, Sir James 9
Maine, Sir Henry Sumner 17,
    139
Maistre, Count Joseph de 78
Manchester 57
Manchesterism 7
Manin, Daniel 84
Manteuffel, Edwin von 80
Marseilles 83
Mazzini, Guiseppe 15, 69, 83–84
medieval revival 83
Metternich, Prince Klemens
    Wenzel Lothar von 80, 82
Mexican field-marshal 54
Mexico 92–93
Middle Ages 93, 108, 135
militancy in Europe 38
militancy 30
Mill, John Stuart 5, 8–11, 13–15,
    19–20, 27, 37, 83, 104, 107,
    131 (note)
minorities 61
monarchy 70, 75–76
monopolies 114
Montagne 46
moral goodness 121
More, Sir Thomas 66

Morely, Lord John 40
Müller, Adam 78
multinational state 15
Mundella, Anthony John 115
Munich 83
Municipal Corporations Act
    (1835) 114
Muratists 79

Naples 92
nation 15, 62, 70, 71–74, 76, 82–
    83, 85–86, 89–90, 92–94, 96,
    100, 102, 107, 110, 147
national identity, sense of 38
national independence 70, 77, 79
national rights 79, 82
national spirit 80
national state/nation-states 15
nationalism 15, 17
nationalities, rights of 69
nationality 69, 74, 77, 79, 81–82,
    83–86, 88–90, 92, 94–96
nationality, theory of 72, 84–85,
    94, 96
nations, collective rights of 72
natural rights 85
Natural Law 17
nature, state of 73
Neapolitan state 92
Netherlands 73
New York 103
Nonconformity 29
Nugent, Count Lavall 82

officaldom 150
Old Mortality Society 24
Old Sarum 105
oligarchy, official 154
orders, representatives of 106
over-legislation 31, 121

Oxford 19, 24

paganism 88
Panhellenism 81
Panslavism 81
Papal Infallibility 15, 17
Paris 38, 73
Paris, university of 88
parliament 22, 31, 97, 116
parliament, members of 20
Parliament (1868) 115
Parliament 98, 101, 104, 106–
    107, 110, 112, 115, 137
Parliament Act (1911) 22, 24
Parliament, Members of 105
parliamentary reform 7, 9, 19–
    20, 113
parliamentary representation 20,
    110
parliamentary system 94–95
Parliamentary Commissions 123
Parliamentary Reformers 98
Parma 92
patriotic attachment, nature of 90
patriotism 19, 22, 36, 79, 86,
    89–90
Paul, Herbert 14
peace treaties 68
Peel, Sir Robert 113–14
Peru, ancient 157
Peter the Hermit 56
Plassy 63
Plato 66
Plotinus 66
Pluralities Bill (1838) 114
Plutocracy 106
Poland 71–72, 80–82, 89
Poles 82
Polish exiles 83
Polish question 79

Polish revolution 81
Polish state 71
power, abuse of 69
power, balance of 98, 103–105, 108, 110
primogeniture 27, 76
production 142, 156
property 69, 75, 119, 125–26
proportional representation 100
Protection 101
Protestantism 67
Protestant countries 74
Prussia 77
public interest(s) 126–28
Public Health Acts 133

race 75, 77, 82–83, 85, 88, 90, 93
races 76, 87, 89, 92–93, 95
rack-renting 112
radical Reformers 97
radicalism 12, 23–24, 29
Radicalism 9, 21, 109
radicals 19
rank, divisions of 33, 54, 137, 142
Reform 98, 104
Reform Act (1867) 26, 105
Reform Bill (1832) 105, 109
Reform, Democratic view of 109
Reformation 67
Reformers 104, 110
regulative agency/agencies 34, 151
regulative apparatus, development of 148
regulative organization 154
regulative structure 150
regulative system 149
regulators 150

religion 13, 15, 37, 77, 81–82, 88–90, 156
religious citizenship 38
religious wars 80
representation 73, 97
representation by orders 108
Republic One and Indivisible 74
republic(s) 71–73, 75, 77, 118
republicanism 73
restoration, anti-national character of 82
Revolt of the Netherlands 67
revolution(s) 56, 68, 72, 74, 77–80, 85–86, 95–96, 146
Rhine, Confederation of 79
Rhone, steam navigation of 38
rights, corporate 70
rights, established 68
rights, national 79
rights, popular 79
rights, private 86
Robinson, Mme Fleury 146
Roman Gaul 75
Roman jurisprudence 76
Roman people 75
Roman republic 74–75
Romans 73
Romans, ancient 88
romantic school 83
Rome 73, 75
Rousseau, Jean-Jacques 69, 91
Royal Commissions 123
royalty 70, 76
rulers, rights of 82
Russia 77
Russians 82

savagery 138
Savoy 83
Saxons 88

Saxony, King of 79
School Boards 116
Schwarzenberg, Prince Felix
    Ludwig Johann Freidrich 80
Scotch Members of Parliament
    107
Scotland 107
Second Reform Act (1867) 35,
    115
Second World War 39
Sects, later medieval 67
self-government 73, 86, 89, 93
serf(s) 139, 141, 143
settlement (1688) 17
settlements, land 125
Sicilian marquis 54
Sidgwick, Henry 40
Sieyès 73
Silesia 71
sinecures, abolition of 114
slave(s) 139, 141-43
slavery 93, 119
small tradesmen 109
Smith, Adam 33
social organization 154
social reform 24-27
social state 68, 154-55
socialism 19, 30-32, 34, 39, 96,
    155-56
socialism, *régime* of 148
Socialism 30
socialist 143-44
socialist despotism 32
socialistic organization 152, 154
society 21, 34, 37, 51, 73, 75,
    88, 90, 118-20, 121, 131,
    137, 139, 141, 148, 150
society, contractual *régime* of 34
society, militant type 142
sovereignty 69, 73

sovereignty of the people 17, 74,
    85
Spain 71, 77, 79, 81, 91
Spanish Bourbons 71
Spencer, Herbert 5, 24, 29-35,
    38, 135-57
state 7, 15, 18, 22, 26, 27, 28,
    29, 34-35, 70, 72, 74, 77,
    83, 86-87, 89-90, 92-95,
    100, 102, 111-112, 116,
    120-22, 124-25, 133, 148
state, British 38
state officialdom 33
state planning 39
state, political functions of 91
state welfare 39
State, law of 121
State, power of 121
State Rights 108
State-interference 123
states 75, 91-93, 95
States, rights of 108
status, *régime* of 32, 143
Stein, Baron Friedrich Karl
    Freiherr von 78
Stephen, James Fitzjames 5, 10-
    14, 17, 19, 23, 36, 46-65
Stephen, Leslie 11
Stephen, Rt Hon. James 10, 11
Stubbs, William 17
suffrage, extension of 20
suffrage, universal 7, 99, 110
Swiss 92
Switzerland 73, 91-92
Talleyrand, Perigord Charles
    Maurice de 79
temperance societies 136
tenant 111-112, 125-29
tenants, protection of 127
tenure, security of 112

Texas 146
tolerance 37
Tories 47
Toryism 31
trade, liberation of 114
trade union(s) 21, 34, 151, 153, 156
tradition 9, 15, 18, 68, 73, 76, 85
Turks 81
Tuscan state 92
tyranny 67, 76, 102
Tyrol 77

Unitarian journals 13
Ultramontanism 14
utilitarianism 9, 25
Utopia 66

Vane, Sir Henry 38
Venice 80
Vergniaud, Pierre Victurnier 73
Vienna 79–81, 83

Vienna, Congress of 80, 81
Vinerian Professor of Law (Oxford) 19

War of Deliverance 79
War of Independence 67
Waterloo 79
Wesleyan 29
Western Europe 74, 88
Western islands 66
Whiggism 9
Whigs 47
Whigs, Holland-House 79
Wittelsbach dynasty 71
women, treatment of 135
worker(s) 33, 143, 150
working conditions, regulation of 27
working men 98, 102–103, 106–107, 109, 151–52
Wycliffe, John 67

Young Italy *see* Giovane Italia

PRIMARY SOURCES IN POLITICAL THOUGHT

This series makes available a number of the important but, until now, inaccessible texts in the history of political thought. Many of these have been over-shadowed by longer or more famous works by the same authors, lost in the obscurity of periodical publication, never translated into English, or simply overlooked or neglected by modern scholars. The series presents the definitive editions of these texts, prepared to the highest standards of contemporary scholarship. These stand as permanent works of reference not only for professional scholars but also for researchers and the general reader.

Already Available

**Liberalism, Democracy, and the State in Britain:
Five Essays, 1862–1891**
Edited and introduced by Julia Stapleton
ISBN 1 85506 534 7 : 168pp : Hb : £25.00 $40.00
ISBN 1 85506 535 5 : 168pp : Pb : £9.95 $15.95

Response to the Paradoxes of Malestroit
Jean Bodin
Translated by Henry Tudor and R. W. Dyson
Introduced by D. P. O'Brien
Notes by J. C. M. Starkey
ISBN 1 85506 532 0 : 177pp : Hb : £32.00 $48.00
ISBN 1 85506 533 9 : 177pp : Pb : £11.95 $19.95

Forthcoming Titles

On the Power of Emperors and Popes
William of Ockham
Translated and introduced by Annabelle Brett
August 1998
ISBN 1 85506 552 5 : Hb
ISBN 1 85506 553 3 : Pb

Forthcoming Titles

The Political Writings of John Wesley
Edited and introduced by Graham Maddox
August 1998
ISBN 1 85506 554 1 : Hb
ISBN 1 85506 555 X : Pb

Founder Editor

Henry Tudor

Editorial Board

R. W. Dyson, Julia Stapleton and **Peter Stirk,** all of the
University of Durham.
The editors gratefully acknowledge the financial support of
the **Publications Board of the University of Durham** in the
preparation of this series.

Thoemmes Press

UK Office
11 Great George Street, Bristol, BS1 5RR, UK

USA Office
22883 Quicksilver Drive, Dulles, Virginia 20166, USA